MISSION *of the* FAMILY

JON LEONETTI

DynamicCatholic.com
Be Bold. Be Catholic.®

MISSION *of the* FAMILY

Printed in the United States of America. [1]

ISBN: 978-1-937509-36-1

Book Design by Shawna Powell

For more information on this title
and other books and CDs available through
the Dynamic Catholic Book Program, please visit:
www.DynamicCatholic.com

The Dynamic Catholic Institute
5081 Olympic Blvd · Erlanger, Kentucky 41018
Phone: 1–859–980–7900
Email: info@DynamicCatholic.com

Table of Contents

"Jon Leonetti's book The Mission of the Family is more than just a solid guide to Church teaching on marriage and the family. It's loaded with personal anecdotes – at times heartwarming and at other times really funny – that show why strong, holy marriages are essential for strong, holy families. Do yourself a favor and read this book!"

CHRISTOPHER WEST
Speaker and Author of *'Fill These Hearts'*

"Blessed John Paul II told families "Become what you are!" Jon Leonetti provides a real glimpse of what that looks like."

CINDY BLACK
Director of Youth, Young Adult & Campus Ministry,
Diocese of Fort Wayne-South Bend

"In a busy society, there is nothing more challenging yet joy-filled than nurturing a holy family. If you've ever hoped for a complete yet easy to understand guide for fostering and maintaining a happy family, this is it!"

TOM PETERSON
President and Founder of Catholics Come Home
and VirtueMedia

Introduction

I am not a priest. I want that to be clear from the beginning. First, because I have such deep respect and profound admiration for the men who serve as our priests, but more important, because I'm writing this book as a husband and father. Of course, I did spend the beginning of my adult life in seminary, and how I got from there to here is a necessary part of this book. The short version, though, is that it had to do with mission. My whole time in seminary I was doing what the Church calls "discernment." We usually think of that as discerning or deciding whether God wants us to be a priest or not. That's part of it, but before a guy can ever get to answering that question he's got to ask a whole lot of other ones. Ultimately he's got to work out what God wants for him specifically. As we'll see, marriage is much the same. What's important for now, though, is that once I came to see what my own sense of mission or purpose truly was, I knew that I hadn't been called to be a priest, and in time I came to see that it had to mean marriage, and not just marriage generally, but marriage *to my wife.*

When I left seminary most people assumed that it had to do with celibacy, that I'd decided that I really wanted to be married and have my own family. The truth was that marriage and family had nothing to do with it. In fact, I left seminary convinced that I would be living the rest of my life as a celibate single layman in the Church. My spiritual director at the time, and a number of other very good priests and professors, cautioned me against making any hasty decisions. Much of this, of course, had come precisely from what I had learned at the seminary.

You see, the biggest thing I think I learned while studying for the priesthood was also the most surprising. It was at seminary that I learned just how hard being a good Christian husband and father is. Family life is a full-time job, and it is not an easy one. There are lots of struggles, lots of failures, and if your faith is important to you, then the stakes are about as high as they can possibly get. Your salvation and the salvation of those closest to you depend upon how well you live your family life together. That's both an awesome responsibility and an incredible burden.

But one thing that has made the burden more bearable and truly helped me in my struggle to become a better husband and father is a sense of meaning and purpose. Even in the Church, sometimes we don't talk very helpfully about what families are for. Sure, during marriage prep we'll say that marriage is for the spouses to grow in holiness and the procreation and education of children, but what's the purpose of having children? What is family life *for*, anyhow? What's the meaning of your family? What's the meaning of your life?

What you may not know, and what I certainly didn't know until I'd been at the seminary for a very long time, is that the Church is very clear on the meaning and purpose of your family. Married couples and families exist for the same reason that priests and religious do: *for mission*. The difference is that while priests and religious communities exist, in some sense, for the service of the Church, we families who live "in the world" exist for the service of that world. What I mean is that our families are the most common and natural representatives of the faith to all those we meet, and we're the most likely source of connection to religion that most of our friends and neighbors of other faiths or without any faith are likely to have. Just stop by any RCIA class or talk to any convert. Most will probably tell you that it wasn't some priest's sermon that brought them in, but the kindness of their neighbor, the generosity they experienced after a tragedy, the devotion of their fiancé, or the changes they saw in a friend's life after her conversion.

Family life is for conversion, the conversion first of the members of the family, and as we continue to strive to grow in holiness, the conversion of all those around us. Family life is for mission, the mission of bringing the good news of the gospel to everyone we meet, and of being the presence of Christ and his Church to those whose lives we touch. So our families are centers of evangelization, sources of grace, and hopefully signs of mercy and compassion. Mostly, if we're doing our jobs well, they are living witnesses to the gospel that has given us, and indeed our very families, life.

The challenges our families face today are greater than ever before, and to make matters worse, many of the supports we've been able to rely on in the past just aren't there anymore. For instance, more than half of parents of newborns now don't live within fifty miles of the child's grandparents. And that's just the beginning. The very values we try and instill in our children, those that are meant to serve as the bedrock of a family's life and mission, are under attack. Worst of all, marriage itself, the solid foundation of traditional family life, fails more often than it succeeds. In the face of such opposition, what's a family to do? How can we even begin to think about mission when just keeping body and soul, husband and wife, parents and kids together under one roof sometimes seems too much?

This book aims to give one answer, or at least to offer some direction to that question. Using my own experience of marriage and family life, the invaluable contacts and associations I have made over many years speaking at Catholic churches, schools, and conferences of every sort, but relying especially on the Church's own teaching and tradition, I hope to provide you with a new sense of mission and purpose for your family life. I hope that you'll see the Church's vision of marriage and family anew, or maybe hear it for the very first time, and be as convinced and converted as I am whenever I hear it. And if that happens, then one thing is certain: Your life and your family's life will never be the same.

Most of all, though, I hope that this little book allows you to hear the voice of God more clearly within your very own family—in your spouse and in your kids, in your own parents and siblings and other near relatives, and within the many complicated relationships that make up your own daily life. You know, we can hear the same message over and over again and never really listen to it. My dad always tells me to check the oil in my car, but I'm not really a car guy, so I usually wait until something else goes wrong with it and take it in to the shop and the mechanic will say, "Man, are you crazy? It's been seven thousand miles since your last oil change!" But if my wife asks me to check the oil, I'm happy to do so. Sometimes life is like that, and we should be glad for those who help us to see things anew.

So let the gospel speak to you anew in the pages that follow, and let yourself be converted again as you were the very first time. Let the turn of your heart set a new course of action for your life, and you'll see that your family is the best chance of success that you have at living, loving, and being the best that you can be. Not only that, but together you'll help others to do the same. In the end, your family will have become your vocation, and your family's vocation will have changed the world.

WE ARE FAMILY

We all think our families are important. In fact, if I asked you what the most important things in your life were you would probably say, "My faith, my family, and my friends," or something like that. I know I would. Most people not only think their own families are important, but that family, as such, is an important ideal or value. However, most of us have a hard time explaining why. Just why are our families so important to us? Why are families important at all?

The Church teaches that the family is "the vital cell of society." Now, this isn't just something clever that some priest in the Vatican thought up over espresso one morning. And it's not something new that they only figured out recently. It turns out that the concept of family is one of the most consistent themes in the whole of the Scriptures. So we'll start there.

THE OLD TESTAMENT

The Old Testament begins with the story of creation. In fact, there are two creation stories at the beginning of the book of Genesis. They each emphasize different things, but the one thing they have in common is placing the creation of humanity as the crown of creation. The first creation story concludes: Then God said: *"Let us make man in our image, after our likeness. Let them have dominion over the fish of the sea, the birds of the air, and the cattle, and over all the wild animals and all the creatures that crawl on the ground." God created man in his image; in the divine image he created him; male and female he created them. God blessed them, saying: "Be fruitful and multiply; fill the earth and subdue it."* (Gen. 1:26–28)

So the human person is the high point of creation because the human person, of all creatures, is made in God's image. But we are created, from the beginning, as male and female. This means that our sexual difference is not only given by God, but is a direct reflection of the divine life. The first commandment that God gives in the Bible is "Be fruitful and multiply," inviting his new creation to participate in the very godly thing that God does: creating new life. This theme is echoed in the second creation story:

The LORD God formed man out of the clay of the ground and blew into his nostrils the breath of life, and so man became a living being. Then the LORD God planted a garden in Eden, in the east, and he placed there the man whom he had formed. The LORD God said: "It is not good for the man to be alone. I will make a suitable partner for him." So the LORD God formed out of the ground various wild animals and various birds of the air, and he brought them to the man to see what he would call them; whatever the man called each of them would be its name. The man gave names to all the cattle, all the birds of the air, and all the wild animals; but none proved to be the suitable partner for the man. So the LORD God cast a deep sleep on the man, and while he was asleep, he took out one of his ribs and closed up its place with flesh. The LORD God then built up into a woman the rib that he had taken from the man. When he brought her to the man, the man said: "This one, at last, is bone of my bones and flesh of my flesh; This one shall be called 'woman,' for out of 'her man' this one has been taken." That is why a man leaves his father and mother and clings to his wife, and the two of them become one body. The man and his wife were both naked, yet they felt no shame. (Gen. 2:7, 18–25)

The first creation story highlights the importance of humanity by making it the capstone of creation, the last and best thing God makes. The second story does it by making the man the first thing that God creates, and the importance of the male-female dynamic is captured in the creation of the woman, who is made not out of the earth like the man, but out of his own flesh and blood. In both stories the message is clear: The most important thing that God creates is the human person; in fact, the whole of creation is, in a certain sense, for them. The great dignity of humanity consists in being made in the image and likeness of God, and this image and likeness is shown most perfectly not in the human being all alone, but together in a sexual union that allows them both to fulfill the first commandment, to be fruitful and multiply. The message of those first Scriptures is clear: The human person is made for family.

But families are not perfect. From the beginning Adam and Eve, our first parents, are something of a mixed bag. It is their sin that drives humanity from the paradise of Eden, and their own sin affects—we might even say infects—their children so much that the first murder takes place not between strangers or rival soldiers or bitter enemies, but between brothers. God's first great intervention in human history is to save a particular family, that of Noah, during the days of the Great Flood. Most of what follows reads like dead space in the Scriptures because it consists largely of lists—lists and lists and lists . . . of families. *This is the record of the descendants of Terah. Terah became the father of Abram, Nahor, and Haran, and Haran became the father of Lot,* and so on. The names might sound foreign to us now, but this is really not so different from the stories that many of us tell around the kitchen table: "Tom and Beth had Sarah back in '82, but that was before they lived in the old house on Seventh . . ." The Scriptures tell the very same sort of story that we tell today, but the scriptural story is there to help us understand our own story.

The importance of family starts to really crystallize, however, when God finally chooses a family of his own. Abram, who began as just another of the names in the ancient lists, is called by God to leave home and family to start his own family anew in a distant land. In so doing he becomes Abraham, the father of the Hebrew people. Abraham's story is all about family. He and his wife, Sarah, are infertile. God promises a son but since Sarah is past menopause Abraham presumes that the son must come from someone else. He uses a surrogate named Hagar and has a son by her, whom he calls Ishmael. The familiar story of Abraham taking his son Isaac to be sacrificed to God is usually told to illustrate the importance of faith even in difficult circumstances, but it is just as much a story of family. Abraham's heart is breaking for the whole of the story because he is being asked to give up what is most precious to him—his own son. Of course, for us Christians, this is a kind of preview or foreshadowing of what God himself is going to do in the sacrifice of his own son, Jesus. But even on its own the story of God's choosing the Hebrew people is a powerful testimony to his care for, love of, and devotion to families.

THE NEW TESTAMENT

We call the mystery by which God himself took on human flesh and entered into the human story the Incarnation. This literally means the "enfleshment" of the Lord. While this can sometimes confuse us, Jesus is God; he always was God, and it was as God, from all eternity, that he entered into time in the womb of Mary. He was born into the world like any other human baby, and in so doing he accepted a whole family history. Think of all those long lists of names we read in the Gospels around Christmastime: "And so-and-so begat such-and-such." These are the real live people who were Jesus's grandparents and great-grandparents and great-great-grandparents. And just like your great-granddaddy might have been a bootlegger or a thief or a cowboy, Jesus's family tree is full of spotty fruit too. But in accepting this whole family history Jesus shows us two things: first, that even this history is important, or else the lists would have been left out; and second, that great goodness can be found in even the most dysfunctional of families.

It's important to remember just what kind of a family situation Jesus was born into. The Holy Family was first of all blended; at the very least Jesus was not the biological child of Joseph, and as the tradition has it that Joseph was previously married there is a good chance that "the brothers of the Lord" whom we meet later in the Gospels were Jesus's stepbrothers from Joseph's first marriage. This isn't just pious tradition, either. The word *adelphoi*, which is what the Gospel writers used for "brothers," in this case means "brothers," "brothers and sisters," "cousins," and "anyone like my brother." However Jesus was related to these people, the Holy Family was not a conventional one and probably wouldn't even stand up to the scrutiny of many of our parishes.

Jesus is himself the result of an unplanned pregnancy, and to top it all off his family was homeless at the time of his birth. Shortly after this they became refugees, probably something very much like today's illegal immigrants fleeing from a corrupt political situation. This is important because in his story Jesus is completely set apart from all other gods of the people. The heroes of the pagans always come from noble bloodlines and have exalted family stories—even the Buddha was born a prince—but only in the Christian story do we have a God born as a pauper.

Jesus, simply by being who he is, reveals the two greatest mysteries of God. We have already mentioned the first: how it is that Jesus can be at once both fully God and fully man. If that paradox is too much for you, then just hold on to your seat. The great mystery that lives at the heart of God is this: God is himself both one and three. This is the mystery we Christians call the Blessed Trinity. I know, I know, it seems remote and unrelated. I pray to God, and probably the way I pray to God wouldn't change very much whether God was a Trinity or not, but it does affect the way you relate to God, and hopefully the way we relate to each other.

Because we typically talk about the Trinity in terms of the "One in Three" or the "Three in One," people tend to think it's all about numbers. It's not. The Trinity is all about relationship. In fact, the whole point of the Trinity is that God lives in relationship with himself. The Trinity is not simply a helpful way for us to understand God, but is the way God actually is. God the Father, from all eternity, actually is Father. He does what fathers do: He fertilizes, he begets, he creates, he cares for, and he sustains. God the Son, who is Jesus, is the son from all eternity. Jesus doesn't become God's son at some point in his life, nor does God become son when Jesus is born of Mary; God the Father relates to himself as Son, and that bond of relationship, that perfect love, is the Holy Spirit. This is a great mystery—the greatest of mysteries, in fact—and philosophers and theologians have argued for centuries about how best to talk about it. That's not terribly important for us. What is important is that God is a sort of family, even before we know him; before anything at all is created God lives in bonds of love with himself.

So God freely chooses to enter into human history as a particular man, born to a particular family, as a member of a particular tribe, itself part of a particular nation. The Jewish people were always conscious of their divine election—the fact that God had chosen them from among all the peoples of the earth—to be holy. They developed and cultivated complex codes of ritual purity and observance, and even shunned outsiders as unclean. Strangely, however, while Jesus was undeniably Jewish, he freely broke this "holiness code" as he saw fit, and he associated openly with sinful Jews: tax collectors, prostitutes, and fringy religious types. Most important for us, he befriended pagans.

While the Jews had a long history of recognizing certain Gentiles or non-Jews as righteous, cooperating openly and freely with them was never an option. What's more, righteous Gentiles were typically Jewish in belief but not by birth. These pagans whom Jesus helped were pagan Romans and Greeks. The Romans were even the political force occupying the country at the time. Even for the most unobservant Jew this was basically treason, and it is to one of these that Jesus gives the highest praise in the whole of the New Testament: *"Never in all of Israel have I found such faith."* (Matt. 8:10)

This, again, is extremely important, because it is in Jesus that God seems to be at once validating the particular call of the Jewish people and extending that call to the whole world. This is why

Saint Paul can write only a few years after Jesus's death, *Through faith you are all children of God in Christ Jesus. For all of you who were baptized into Christ have clothed yourselves with Christ. There is neither Jew nor Greek, there is neither slave nor free person, there is not male and female; for you are all one in Christ Jesus. And if you belong to Christ, then you are Abraham's descendant, heirs according to the promise.* (Gal. 3:26–29)

The special bond God shared with Israel and cemented in Jesus is, by faith in Jesus, shared with the whole world. This matches well what Jesus said in his own teaching on the family. Though devoted to his mother, seeing to her needs even to the end on the cross, he was not afraid to teach:

> *While he was still speaking to the crowds, his mother and his brothers appeared outside, wishing to speak with him. (Someone told him, "Your mother and your brothers are standing outside, asking to speak with you.") But he said in reply to the one who told him, "Who is my mother? Who are my brothers?" And stretching out his hand toward his disciples, he said, "Here are my mother and my brothers. For whoever does the will of my heavenly Father is my brother, and sister, and mother." (Matt. 12:45–48)*

Jesus affirms the primacy and importance of the family, but turns the criteria for family relationships upside down. "Family" is no longer simply those people related to you by blood, though hopefully it will include them too. Instead God's own family is made up of those who share faith in Christ Jesus.

GOD'S FAMILY

The whole story of God's relationship with humanity is about making us part of his family. Though we are born into our natural families in a natural way, we are born into God's supernatural family in a supernatural way. Baptism is the birth of water and the Holy Spirit, which allows us to be members of God's family. Jesus is God's son by birth, but we are God's sons and daughters by baptism. This doesn't make us any less God's children than Jesus, however. In fact, if anything, just as Jesus is more Son to the Father than any human son is to his own father, so too by baptism we are more son or daughter to God than we are even to our own parents.

From the first moment the Lord saw that it was not good for the man to be alone, the family of humanity has been growing. And since the risen Jesus gave his great commission to his followers to teach and baptize all nations, the family of God, the Church, has been spreading to people of every nation, language, and way of life. The family of God is the most inclusive family imaginable because it aims to include absolutely everybody. And this same God not only allows us but *expects* us to be part of that great expansion. He demands not only that each of us, to the best of our ability, and our families all together be a sign of this huge, expansive, inclusive family of God but also that we go out into the highways and byways to bring as many along with us as we can.

And so the story goes: Once God chose a man so that he might choose all men. Once God raised up a tribe so that he could gather all the tribes of the earth. Once God raised up a single nation so that he might draw all nations to himself. Once God chose a family so that he might make all families his. Once upon a time God became man, so that through that man you might become part of God's family too.

A FIRM FOUNDATION

If you're like me, math never came easy, either in high school or in college. Oh, I can add and subtract, multiply and divide, balance my checkbook and make out a budget, but anything beyond that and things start to get a little bit fuzzy. Sine and cosine and tangents and all the rest—it was all more confusing than cool. I think it was algebra that first threw me. I must have missed the day when they told us that letters were now going to be numbers. But eventually I got it, and it actually did get me to see math in a whole new way.

We Christians have a kind of algebra of our own. The two great mysteries of the Christian faith, the Incarnation and the Trinity, have everything to do with numbers, but what we do with numbers when talking about God is altogether different from what we do with numbers when talking about anything else. In the mystery of the Incarnation, Jesus, who is God, becomes a man. And yet he doesn't stop being God to do so. We say that he has two "natures," or states of being, but that Jesus himself remains one person. This is a confusing teaching. It's hard to understand, maybe even harder to explain, but most Christians the world over and throughout history have been able to grasp it. And if you think that one's tough, then just try on the Trinity for size. The whole foundation of Christian faith rests on this:

There is one God. It's what separates the three great monotheistic religions—Judaism, Islam, and Christianity—from all the rest. And yet we Christians, unlike the other two, weirdly insist that this one God who is more one than anything else is one, is at one and the same time three.

So it seems that "funny math" lies at the very foundation of the faith. It shouldn't surprise us, then, that it also serves as the basis for marriage and family life. Remember when Jesus was asked about marriage?

> He said in reply, "Have you not read that from the beginning the Creator 'made them male and female' and said, 'For this reason a man shall leave his father and mother and be joined to his wife, and the two shall become one flesh' so they are no longer two, but one flesh. Therefore, what God has joined together, no human being must separate." (Matt. 19:4–6)

In a marriage two become one. This serves as the basis for a healthy, holy family. In order for three or more people to become one family it is first necessary for two individuals to become one flesh. In order for three to become one, two must first become one. In order for a family to be as authentic and wholesome and holy as it can be, it is first necessary for a couple to be as authentic and wholesome and holy as they can be. In other words, marriage is the foundation for every family.

YOU CAN'T GIVE WHAT YOU DON'T HAVE

There is a very famous Latin phrase that a priest-professor of mine used to use back at college: *Nemo dat, quod non habet*. Basically it translates to "You can't give what you don't have." Father used to use this phrase on me all the time: from the pulpit, in the confessional, and especially in class. It's a great phrase, and if you haven't heard it then I want you to memorize it right now. You can't give what you don't have. You can't give what you don't have. You can't give what you don't have. *You can't give what you don't have.*

Think about it for a second: Can you teach a skill you haven't first learned yourself? Can you donate money to a charity that you haven't made yet? Can you offer time to help out your neighbor if you haven't first put in the time at work? Can you help your kids to love your spouse, their siblings, and one another if you don't first show them how to do so yourself? This principle applies virtually everywhere, but nowhere so well as in family life.

Most of the things that we struggle with in our families boil down to this principle. Think about the financial problems you and your spouse and your family have struggled with, or may be struggling with currently. We want to give our spouses and our kids absolutely everything: the best education, the best health care, the best opportunities, the best books, the best toys, the best technology; but few of us can afford the best even some of the time, let alone all of it. Or think about time, which if you're like me is your most precious commodity, and the one your family sometimes gets last. Most of us don't spend enough time with our families, and we don't do ourselves any favors by making promises that we can't keep. Genuine change is required. Of course, if we don't spend enough time with our families, then what we need to do is manage our time better. If we don't make enough money to do what we want to do, we need to either adjust our projected level for attaining "happiness" or better budget our finances. In our families today, we must be willing to make a concentrated effort to have everything we need so that we are able to give freely to the people who need it most.

But perhaps this little philosophical gem works best in the context of relationships. We can't give love unless we've first learned to receive it. And we can't teach love until we've first learned to show it. Again, for this reason a truly holy family is built not only on the firm foundation of faith, but on the brick and mortar of a healthy marriage.

THE HEART OF THE MATTER

We usually think of courtship, romance, and marriage as essentially matters of the heart, and certainly they are that. But when these relationships transition into family life, what we often miss is that the "heart" of a family remains the marriage between the couple. We emphasize and prioritize the relationship between parents and children, but we often forget to look at the first relationship: that between husband and wife, who each in turn become father and mother. Our identities shift over time, and certainly becoming a mother or a father is an unalterable and life-changing event, but one thing we mustn't ever forget is that mothers and fathers are first wives and husbands.

The bond of love that unites husband and wife is precisely the bond of love that will unite a family. Difficulties between the parents can certainly signal difficulties within the family itself, and struggles between other members can most often be linked back to problems between the couple. Now, none of this is meant to be judgmental; this surely doesn't mean that every family who experiences the pain of separation or divorce is some kind of failure, or that because Mom and Dad don't get along very well we're bad people. In fact, some of my friends who have experienced the pain of divorce within their families have turned out kinder and happier than some of my friends who haven't. Ultimately what this is meant to help us understand, especially for those married couples just starting out, is that the best gift that we can give to our children is to love our spouse as truly, madly, deeply, and absolutely as we can.

Likewise, the best gift that we can give to our spouse is to be the best parent that we can be. Our roles as husband and father, wife and mother are inextricably interlinked. But being the best person that we can be and struggling to succeed at the hard work of growing a relationship (whether it's with our spouse, kids, in-laws, or other family members) is our best chance of success across the board.

FALL IN LOVE, STAY IN LOVE

We sometimes think of "falling in love" as a onetime event. If I'm living my marriage as authentically as I can, however, I should fall more deeply in love with my wife, not just once, but every single day of my life. Growing up I served Mass a few times for a priest who read this little inscription that was on one of the cabinets in the sacristy before Mass. It went something like this:

> Priest of God,
>
> say this Mass,
>
> as if it were
>
> your first Mass,
>
> your last Mass,
>
> your only Mass.

Though I didn't realize it at the time, he was teaching me even then about my future responsibilities as a husband and father. For the priest, "married" to the Church, tends his best when he feeds and cares for her, as in the Mass. This foreshadowed for me what my life would eventually be with Teresa. My wife has been such a gift to me that since then I've adopted something of the same mantra for our life together. To be honest, it began with making love, but nowadays I say it as something of a prayer each morning before I get out of bed:

Man of God,

live your life

with your wife/kids

this day, as if it were

your first day with them,

your last day with them,

your only day with them.

Be attentive to your spouse. Keep up with his life, take an interest in his interests (even if they're not your own—maybe especially then). Men, that may mean that rather than sitting down and waiting for your wife to finish her shopping you walk with her (stop rolling your eyes). Women, it may mean sitting down to watch that dreaded football game that takes up your husband's entire Sunday afternoon. (Don't put down the book yet!) But it certainly doesn't stop there. I knew an old couple who kept going on dates every Saturday evening until his death. They were married for more than sixty-five years! She later told me that it was because of their commitment to these "date nights" that their marriage lasted through their most trying times. His humor and silliness toward the waitstaff, she recounted, even up until the week he died, was one of the main things that kept her smiling through it all.

Falling in love takes more work after you really get to know the person. You know her faults intimately now in a way that you didn't before. But over time you can come to love her in spite of and even for the faults. This is one of the things that amaze me so much about love in general. For instance, Teresa knows me better than anyone. And through it all she loves me. In my best and at my worst, she cares for me. Whether I'm speaking in front of five thousand people, with nice clothes and gelled hair (or lack thereof), or waking up next to her with stinky breath and crusty eyes, she loves me! It's amazing and at the same time humbling.

The point is, the most important thing that you can do for your spouse, for your kids, for your family, for your life, is to love each other as best you can, and to show that love in both the darkest and happiest of times. It's not easy, but then again, Christ never promised it would be.

SCHOOL OF VIRTUE

John Paul II called the family "the school of virtue." The rite of baptism of infants calls the parents "the first teachers of their children" in the ways of the faith. Parents are called to pass on to their children the best of what they've been given, and yes, to help them learn from their mistakes. Parents are to teach their children more than just information—they are to teach them transformation. Parents model for their children what life in the Spirit really looks like, and by their example as much as anything else show their kids what it means to be a Christian day in and day out.

The family is the place where we learn about social graces. This isn't just about what kind of silverware to use and where to put our napkins, but about how to treat other people. Parents, therefore, have a special obligation to be as virtuous as they can be. Your kids are going to learn from you how to treat poor people. Your sons will learn how to treat the girls they date by how you treat your wife and daughters. Your daughters will learn what to expect from the men in their lives by the way their fathers and brothers act. And to be honest, the more I speak at high schools across the country, the more important I believe this is.

The most important school your kids will ever attend is at the kitchen table, in the living room, and out in the backyard of your family home. Your kids will learn from how you treat each other how they are supposed to treat other people. In the school of virtue there is but one teacher, though there are some who are further along in the curriculum than others. Of course, over time, and as they age, our kids teach us about virtue too. They make us better, not only by how they challenge us but also by the example they offer. We've all heard it said that "life has its fair share of lessons for those who are willing to take note," or something like that. Sometimes people talk about the "school of hard knocks." Well, any authentically human life is going to have some real suffering in it, some genuinely hard knocks, but it should also have some real graces.

There is, of course, no graduating from the school of virtue, just as there's no vacation from your vocation. The kids grow up and leave the house, but the couple is still left together. What we typically call "empty nest syndrome" is often a great opportunity to grow in virtue in a new way. This is true for the widowed too, even if it looks like theirs is primarily an independent study. Not only that, but even serious failures in the school of virtue can wind up being opportunities for sanctification.

DUNCE CAPS, CORNERS, AND SITTING IN DETENTION

Of course, one of the major problems with any school is discipline. It's not an accident that *discipline* and *disciple* are nearly the same word. A disciple is like a student, but something more: a groupie, a hanger-on, even a wannabe. But to be a faithful disciple, to be a good student in the school of virtue, requires a lot of discipline and hard work, and often enough it entails failure. Mostly those failures are small enough—quick tempers and thoughtless actions, chores left undone and toilet seats left up. But sometimes they're serious, and when they're very serious, then something needs to be done.

In school, if someone messes up a little bit he gets a warning or some small punishment. If it's a relatively serious infraction then he gets detention (and believe me, I know a little something about that). A number of detentions results in a visit to the principal's office and eventually suspension, a last resort before expulsion. The Church's disciplinary code operates more or less the same way, and in our families we do the same sort of thing. We offer gentle correction and rebuke as the kids misbehave, time-outs for more serious mistakes, and removal of privileges for the most serious mistakes. Ultimately we may need to meet with a counselor or a priest. But what happens when the wrongdoer isn't one of the children but is one of the parents? What do you do if your husband is addicted to porn? What if your wife really can't be trusted with the credit card? What if a real problem like infidelity, alcoholism, or drug addiction rears its ugly head? How

31

do you suspend or expel someone from a marriage?

Secular society takes divorce far too lightly. Prime-time sit-coms treat us to family units in which formerly married people can raise kids in perfect harmony and remain close friends. Of course, in real life this almost never happens. Divorce is ugly, and though it might sometimes be necessary, someone always gets hurt. Usually for the divorce to happen it means somebody has already been hurt, and usually very badly.

Though Jesus clearly didn't approve of divorce, we in the Church are not immune to its effects. The divorced, whether re-married or not, whether their marriages have been annulled or not, fill our churches and therefore our homes. My father was divorced at a very young age, and though he is still married to my mother, I have seen and heard the deeply difficult effects the divorce has had on him. He is very open about them, and through his openness I have become all the more attentive to those I serve in parishes and schools across the country. You as well may have personally experienced the effects of divorce, or know someone who has. They are our brothers and sisters and sons and daughters and friends and neighbors and all the rest. And they deserve our love and respect, because they are about very difficult work, and they need all the support they can get.

The children of divorced couples demand our special attention as well, because the natural support of the family has become so terribly disrupted. Obviously each situation is different and needs to be treated as such, but as a rule families, friends, and parishioners need to be as helpful and supportive as they can, especially when it comes to the children, who are not only the parents' responsibility but that of the whole community. This is what being Catholic is all about.

One of the toughest things about divorce is that the former spouses have to figure out how to live continuing to relate to each other, especially with regard to the kids. Some feel angry and betrayed, even if no marital infidelity occurred. Clearly it's impossible to love in the way a person once did, but—and this is a hard saying, I know—the love cannot end, not absolutely. If for no other reason than this is your kid's parent, you have to find a way to respect him for what you can, to love him in spite of your differences, and to put first and foremost the welfare of your kids. Now, of course this isn't easy, and it involves failure, just as before. It also presumes that you're dealing with a relatively rational, stable person, which you may or may not be. Obviously if your former spouse is a danger to you or your kids, then out of love for her as well as for your children, you have to keep her away for her own good as well as for the kids'. But pretending that divorce is no big deal is a nonstarter, and resolving to hate your ex's guts for the rest of your life will likewise not prove very helpful. In the end, there's no graduating from the school of virtue, even if you change classrooms.

FROM THE FEW COME THE MANY

The Church was born from the faith of a few in the experience that they had of the resurrected Lord. The eleven were sent out after the Lord's resurrection to preach the good news and their witness was strengthened by the support of the other disciples who had known and seen Jesus in his life, death, and resurrection. Though they started small and had many bumps along the way, this ragtag group of individuals became the greatest religious movement and the strongest force for good in the history of the world.

As daunting as it sounds, we are all called to do the same in our own families. It starts with the faith of just two, a husband and wife together, and together their daily witness and constant example of striving for good, failing, and striving yet again is what will make or break the faith they are passing on to their children. When Teresa and I were trying for a child our prayer was first that it was God's will, and second that he would give us the grace to be saints, in order to then help our children to be saints. A family sent on mission is born first from a couple committed to their vocation. Of course, the first converts they are to make are themselves. It all begins with us.

So think about those ways in which you can better and more perfectly engage God, both as individuals, as a couple, and especially as a family. How can you more consciously make the love of the Trinity the solid ground of your marriage, your care of your kids, and the relationships in your extended family? How can those relationships, those expressions of communion, and that deep love that your neighbors know and see in you make more manifest the faith you profess and the love you bear? In the end, how can you help your friends and neighbors to see the "something more" that could change the course of their lives?

GOD'S FAMILY

Jesus came to reveal God in the context of a family relationship. He, as son, came to reveal God as father. But Jesus didn't simply reveal God as father to him, but rather God the Father as father. In order to accomplish this he sent the Holy Spirit and established the Church so that we could experience God as our father too. Through the words and actions of Jesus, God's family comes to extend beyond the persons of the Trinity to the Church, which is where those words and actions are still celebrated. And through the Church, which is God's family here on earth, the presence and love and grace of that family reach out to touch the whole world.

A lot of people today think that the way we talk about God as father is a kind of fancy metaphor, even if it was a metaphor given by Jesus. But, they point out, that image fails if you've had a bad relationship with your earthly father. This has even led some to rename the Trinity. No longer would we have Father, Son, and Holy Spirit, but Creator, Redeemer, and Sanctifier, or some other strange configuration of three names that may have something vaguely to do with God

The trouble with these new names, and really with the whole exercise, is that they miss just the way in which God relates to us as Father, as Son, and as Holy Spirit. Jesus is the Son of God by his birth in time of Our Lady, but from all eternity he is God the Son. This means that Jesus, the Word, God the Son, participated in the creation of the world, ages before his own birth in time. Likewise the Father and the Holy Spirit were present for all of Jesus's earthly ministry, which means they both participated in the redemption. What is important about the names of the persons of the Trinity is that they are not mostly about how God relates to us, but about how God relates to himself. This is how the persons of the Trinity relate to each other. The Son is begotten by the Father from all eternity, the Father is eternally begetting, the Spirit constitutes the eternal bond of love between the two. All of this is basically fancy God-talk for "This is what God is really like, and in Jesus we get to participate in it directly." We do so through the community he left us (the Church), and the help he gave us (the sacraments).

The Church is God's family. We are made by grace what Jesus is by birth, and not only his birth in time by Mary, but his "birth" by the Father in eternity. This is why in the Creed we say, "born of the Father before all ages," and why we call him the "only begotten." Jesus shares his sonship with us by grace, which is communicated in the sacraments celebrated by the Church. For most Christians, the normal place of encounter with God through these sacraments, and so the "house" where God's family gathers, is the local parish church.

THE FAMILY HOME

As children we were probably told that the Church is "God's house." If we complained about dressing up or having to be quiet someone probably told us this, and it shut us up just as surely as if we were going to Grandma's. Well, we should have a certain respect for the Church just as we would for Grandma's house, but we should feel comfortable there too. Think of going to Mass like sitting at the feet of Grandpa telling us a story. We go there because God is there in a way he isn't in our house, even though he is surely in our house too. And just as we get from Grandpa a sense of identity and community and what it means for us to be us, so also at Mass we learn what it means to be part of this family, the family that gathers at this house, has these stories, and shares in this meal.

The church building itself is important for just this reason. I'm from Iowa, and with more and more people moving from small towns into the city, and fewer and fewer priests to cover the parishes in the outlying areas, many churches have simply had to close. You've never seen pain until you've seen a thick-chested, full-bearded, rough-handed farmer weep that the church his great-grandfather helped to build, the building where he and everyone he knew was baptized, confirmed, received first Holy Communion, was married, and where he expected to be buried, has to be dismantled stone by stone. And yet that pain is good, at least inasmuch as it shows how important these places become to us. It's not that the building is special or sacred for the stuff in it, though obviously there's real value there too, but because of what happens in it. The building reminds us, like an old house, of all the family gatherings, special celebrations, and impromptu occasions that make up our lives together—our lives together as family.

You hear a lot of talk these days about what you ought to wear to Mass. This isn't totally crazy, since I grew up in a generation in which "anything goes" was considered the best policy (I once saw a lady show up to help distribute Communion in a green tube top and leather miniskirt). We should dress up for Sunday Mass, and we should make sure that we're preparing ourselves, both on the inside and on the outside, to go meet God. At the same time, though, we should feel comfortable enough with the space and with the people in it that we could show up anytime. Yes, I like wearing shorts more than anyone, but we have a responsibility to evangelize, even through the way we dress, to each person in the pew. What are we saying by what we wear?

QUALITY TIME

When you think about it, our homes are sacred or special for the same reason. Sure, we might like a particular view or the setup of a given room, but what we really prize about a place, and the reason that sometimes our favorite houses are the least expensive, is what happened there, and the people who shared the experience. Our families, friends, and neighbors are the people with whom we share our lives and so the experience of our homes. Though the phrase isn't super helpful and has definitely been abused, it's also accurate: *Quality time*, not necessarily quantity time, is what really counts.

Our homes are where we celebrate and suffer the events of daily life. They are where we eat and where we sleep, where we bathe and where we dress. We put on parties in our living rooms and get ready to go out in our bedrooms. We shine shoes, press slacks, wipe down counters, mop floors, vacuum carpets, and dust bookshelves. We mow the lawn, trim the hedge, clean out the gutters, and unclog drains. We get sick and hold our kids when they get sick. We snuggle up on the couch and read books on the porch. We hurry home for our favorite show and sometimes just veg on the couch. We receive news of a death and word on that promotion, phone calls from far away and hollers over the back-yard fence. We open presents under the tree, dress the turkey, lay out the tablecloth, grill out back, and sometimes shovel the walk. Our homes are where our life happens, and the circle of people who make up that life are the people that exist in and around our own homes. These times become quality time, not only because of what we're doing together, but because of the people with whom we're doing them.

The Church is no different. We go there for life-changing cel-ebrations and daily reassurances. Our parishes are where we cel-ebrate Christmas and Easter and Pentecost and the third Sunday of Ordinary Time and the Feast of Saint Whatshername from the Republic of Some Other Place. If we're fortunate enough to have a parish school and we can afford to send our kids there, we celebrate everything from kindergarten and eighth grade gradu-ation to Letter Day and field trips. The parish church is where we spend our lives, day after day, week after week, year after year. Hopefully the relationships we have there are some of the most important in our lives. Maybe even more important, hopefully those relationships that are already some of the most important become something even more in and through the Church. For example, I know a woman who was marrying a guy whom her parents did not like at all. Chief among their concerns was that he wasn't a Catholic; in fact, he wasn't much of anything at the time. He converted more or less for convenience at first, but one year he and his father-in-law volunteered to take over the yard work at the parish. Somehow tending the lawn and trees up there on the weekends changed something in both of them. Now the father, who had actually refused to come to the wedding, is best friends with his son-in-law. Most of our stories won't be quite that dramatic, but taking our natural relationships to a supernatural level can yield results that right now we couldn't possibly imagine.

FAMILY MEALS

There are family meals and then there are *family meals.* You know the difference. A husband and wife and their kids might eat dinner together every night of the week, or at least most nights, hopefully. But on Sundays something special might happen: Whether the gathering is at the same table or somewhere else, Grandma and Grandpa, maybe some aunts or uncles, cousins, and a neighbor or two get thrown in, and the family circle is widened. That meal celebrates a sense of identity that is every bit as intimate as what the nuclear family does each night, but at the same time it's more expansive. For most families, holidays are like this but supersized.

It shouldn't surprise us, then, that the central focus of the Church's life is a family meal. In fact, given Jesus's whole family-based revelation of God, it shouldn't surprise us that the sacrifice he left us as a memorial of his life, death, and resurrection is, in fact, a family meal. The analogy isn't perfect, but we can view, in a certain way, daily Mass as something like dinner every night with the family, Sunday Mass like Sunday dinner at Grandma's, and holy days like holidays with the family.

Much as with regular old family meals, we need to make sure our kids have an experience of each. Christmas, Easter, other holy days—these should basically be nonnegotiable. Sundays should be simply expected as a regular practice. While daily Mass needn't have the same place in your family's life as the family dinner, you really should think about giving your kids the experience of daily Mass in much the same way you'd like to make sure they have the experience of Tuesday evening dinner with Grandpa.

IT'S ALL IN THE FAMILY

If family is the principal metaphor for understanding God in terms of his own internal life in the Trinity, then it should come as no surprise that "family" is the best way of thinking about the Church as well. From the pope on down the Church is one great "family of God," as the documents of Vatican II say, and so the local parish, as a sort of microcosm, is a little local snapshot of God's own family.

The relationships in the Church should parallel, if not perfectly, at least mostly, the relationships in your own family. Think about the people at your local parish. the old lady who does the linens, the gentleman who always reads at Mass (that's my dad), the choir director who sings off-key, and the usher who always seems more interested in where people are sitting or standing than in what Father is saying or how we're all praying. Isn't this awfully like Grandma needing her hair done each Friday, Uncle Bill always reading the sports reports, that cousin from California who always brings the guitar and can't sing to save his soul, Aunt Susie who talks really loud, and the cousin who comes over and spends his time texting and not talking to anybody? Right there in your own parish you have everything that you have in your family, and probably most any kind of person that anyone has in their family.

Consider Father, for example. The role of the priest is perhaps the most confused in the whole Church. The pastor is obviously the "head parent" of the family. Along with the other priests, if there are any, he is the "head of the household" and leader of the family. We trust Father to lead the family well, to answer questions honestly, and to be a good sounding board and wisdom figure for the rest of us. This doesn't make Father perfect, and it certainly doesn't mean that we can never disagree with him, but it does mean our relationship with him demands respect, and that we have a duty to care for him. Just like with our parents and grandparents, it demands that we offer our care for him, whether we like him personally or not.

This is why it's important that Catholics (and Orthodox Christians) call their priests "Father." Our priests aren't just the Catholic equivalent of a Protestant minister or a sort of rabbi. Our priests are heads of the household of God as it exists in our local parish. Their role is more like that of the head of a household in ancient Israel than the rabbis of old or of today. They are teachers, it's true, and they do offer a sacrifice and are therefore priests, but they are mostly fathers in a spiritual family. He helps give birth to new children in Christ by baptism, whether they're infants or adults. He confirms them in their faith and gifts them with the Spirit as they grow. He witnesses their marriage, helps those who need to discern find their way to the altar. He visits and anoints the sick, prepares the elderly for death, and reconciles the hardest of hearts with God. He witnesses to the love married couples have for each other. Most fundamentally, he feeds us, literally with the body and blood of the Lord. And if he means it, he shares his own body and blood too, just like a father who works long and hard hours for his family.

There are, of course, other leaders in the parish. If you live in a big enough city and belong to a large enough parish, then your pastor may still be fortunate enough to have an assistant or two on staff. Other priests, whether they are young and learning the ropes or older but still relatively active, can be a real treasure of

ROB & VICKI MATCHETT
951-779-3021
800-922-7362

Rob & Vicki Matchett
CLOSE COVER BEFORE STRIKING

Matchett Real Estate Group

"We Match Buyers & Sellers"

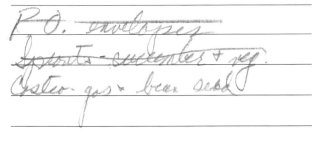

P.O. envelopes

~~Sprints - sweeten~~ + reg.

Oyster - gas + bean seed

_____

_____

_____

_____

_____

_____

_____

_____

spiritual wealth. Men and women religious, nuns, sisters, and religious brothers are something like aunts and uncles, or wise old cousins who are able to pass on the family's traditions without having to bear the full weight of the responsibility for the community. Permanent deacons and their families are a unique source of both theological knowledge and insight into family life. Some of the holiest men I know are permanent deacons and readily admit that if not for their wives they never would have the faith they do. But whether you live in a one-priest parish or your local parish is headed by a religious community with tons of priests, male and female religious, a slew of deacons, and a staff of dozens, you certainly have the same delightful, insightful, and frustrating mix of people at church that you do in your own family. The point is that, as with your family, you need to work on these relationships with intentionality. This means that you need to spend time at your local parish and their outings, and not just during Sunday Mass. I used to hate going to coffee and doughnuts after Mass. Now I can't get enough of it. And to think it only took that one person who sat with me when I was sitting alone. He introduced me to his family and they introduced me to their friends. Now I try and stay as long as I can, or at least until I eat all the doughnuts.

PUTTING IN THE TIME

Time management is the most frequently reported character flaw today. We've already talked about how hard it is to get just regular time with our family, so spending extra time at church might seem like a genuine impossibility. It doesn't have to be, however, if we make at least part of our family time our church-family time. This presumes regular attendance at Sunday Mass, but it is about something much more essential.

Jesus tells us, *"For where your treasure is, there your heart will be also."* (Matt. 6:21, Luke 12:34) Since time tends to be the most precious commodity for most of us, our treasure is where our time is, and so also where our heart will be. In other words, if you want to see what you really value and prioritize in your life, look at how you spend your time. Most likely work or school make up the bulk of our days, and that's the way it should be. Earning a living and getting an education are two of the most important things that we can do. Probably most of us do have some kind of regular "family time," whether that's every day, every couple of days, or every week. But most of us also have regular shows that we watch, and many of us make a point of exercising every day or two. Perhaps we have hobbies as well that we're faithful to. And don't forget outside friends. If you're reading this book, then Sunday Mass is probably already a regular practice for you, and maybe even weekday Mass sometimes (during Lent, for example). But rather than think of time spent at church as somehow distinct from or over and above time spent with the family, why not try to better incorporate the two?

Of course certain things at church are fairly age specific. If you sit on the parish council, the PTA, the school board, financial committee, or building and grounds, then your seven-year-old probably shouldn't be coming to meetings with you. Likewise, while occasionally visiting your kids' Sunday school classes or Wednesday night catechism might be a good idea, doing so all the time might annoy the teacher. But if you volunteer to work the pancake breakfast, then why not do so as a family? Sure, maybe Mom or Dad has to run the grill, but can't the kids bus tables or pour coffee? Or if there's a car wash to benefit the Boy Scouts or the volleyball team, why not have the younger kids hold the signs and the older kids dry while Mom and Dad run the hoses? The point is that whatever we do with the Church needn't be yet another of the endless list of activities that we do by ourselves. If anything, it should be helping to bring our families closer together.

You've probably heard Father or one of the finance people from your parish talk about "time, talent, and treasure." This is a way to talk about the personal resources each person has, both financial and otherwise, that they can put to the service of the Christian faithful. On a very basic level, if a parishioner owns a lawn care service, then he could offer to cover the parish grounds free of charge or at a reduced rate. More commonly, this is about people recognizing their own gifts and talents and putting those to use in the service of the community, but only those gifts and talents they actually have. For example, if you really can't sing, then don't join the choir (please), but do find something else to do. Because active participation is one of the most important things in the life of the Church, many people begin to do things for which they aren't very well prepared or suited simply because they do not know what to do.

This is all the more true when it comes to time. Spend time with your fellow parishioners. Make sure that your lives intersect somewhere besides Sunday morning Mass. But also make sure that you aren't spending time at church just to put your time in. Strive to see the value of what we do as a Christian people and then desire to spend time with those who hold your values. Show your kids what life in a regular parish is like, and give yourselves the opportunity to learn and grow from your experience of one another.

PUT YOUR MONEY WHERE YOUR MOUTH IS

Nobody likes a fair-weather fan. I love the Cubs, which often gets me into trouble because they don't win as often as they should. But nothing is worse than a person who is only a Cubs fan on the day's they happen to be winning, going to games at Wrigley Field (probably with tickets they scalped off some diehard). If you really care about an ideal, then you'll put your money where your mouth is, and not just when it "feels good". Serious sports fans spend serious money on season tickets, clothing, memorabilia, and the like. Film aficionados spend their money on movie posters and props. Trekkies dress up in special outfits and speak Klingon to each other at conventions. The "treasure" that the Lord was talking about is made up not only of your time, which is money, but also of your money, which is money.

Catholics are notoriously the worst tithers among all Christian denominations. The ancient Jewish custom was to give ten percent of one's income to charity. In many Protestant denominations this is translated into a ten percent donation of one's annual income to the Church. Some churches even ask for tax statements to ensure that their congregants are being honest. But Catholics don't do that. First of all, while ten percent was the ancient Jewish practice, it has never been universal in the Christian Church. More important, however, that ten percent didn't simply go to the local synagogue, but represented the whole of one's charitable giving. At the time this mostly meant crop and livestock, which went in part to the upkeep of the priests, but mostly to the care of the poor. So while Catholics typically don't donate ten percent of their gross income to their local parish, they do most often contribute weekly to their local parish, as well as annually to organizations like Catholic Charities, the local Catholic hospital or homeless shelter, seminarian funds, the retirement fund for priests and religious, or even to the care of a local monastery or convent.

The point is a good one, though. Just how do we spend our money as a family? Do my kids see me donate my goods and services to the Church? Do they see my generosity to the poor? Do they see my care for elderly and sick priests and religious? When you're part of a family your financial contributions are not only your own, but that of your whole household. While this certainly means being responsible with the money necessary to care for your children, it also means being responsible with how you form them in the art of charitable giving. And please, do not get wrapped up in the ridiculous notion that the Church is all about your money. The number of people we feed, clothe, care for, and visit far exceeds that of any other institution in the world. In other words, the Catholic Church's charitable action speaks for itself.

EDUCATION FOR LIFE

I travel all around the country, and since I'm always something of an outsider where I speak, people will often say to me, "Jon, I'd really love to be able to send my kids to the local Catholic school if they'd come out with the kind of thing you're talking about, but for what they'd get here, I just can't justify the money." These concerns are always difficult to hear, and not one I can respond to absolutely for anyone. I would, however, like to offer some thoughts.

Parents have an obligation to see to it that their children are raised in the faith and formed in it as best they can be. After all, the Church teaches that the primary teachers of the faith to your children are you, their parents. This is a tough job, however, and comes with many challenges—especially in today's culture. What if the local Catholic school is Catholic in name only? How many problems are too many problems? Do I have some kind of obligation to support the parish school if I can? What do I do if I'm not sure about the religion that my kids would get there? What if I feel like the priest just isn't hearing my concerns?

These are all fair questions that a husband and wife should wrestle with together, and hopefully they will seek some advice from outside sources whom they respect. We do have a general obligation to support the work of the Church, so if the local Church sees educating children at a local parish school as a priority, then we should assist that as best we can. In fact, if we are tithing at all at the local parish, then we are already supporting the parish school, whether we've got kids in it or not. But some Catholic schools, for a whole variety of reasons, are very, very expensive. We aren't under any obligation to endanger our family financially, or take out a second mortgage on our house, or otherwise bring unnecessary disruption to our lives just to send our kids to a Catholic school, especially if the Catholic identity of the school is seriously in question. At the same time, we really need to presume the good in each other and in our institutions. Most of our Catholic schools are extremely good and holy places to educate our kids. They helped to build up the Church in this country and are doing so again. If anything, we should be supporting them now more than ever before.

PROBLEMS IN THE FAMILY

As with any institution or Christian denomination, finances, personnel, management, resources, and just plain old personality conflicts can be a source of real tension and difficulty. We shouldn't expect that just because we are the Church we won't have these kinds of conflicts. However, we should expect from one another that we handle these struggles differently in light of our Catholic faith.

Maybe you don't like the choir director or the grand knight of the local Knights of Columbus council. Or maybe the deacon always talks down to people during his homilies. Or maybe the priest handled a difficult marriage or baptismal situation badly and it hurt someone you love. Or maybe you just think the principal of the parish school is incompetent. Or that the school lunch is bad. Or that the confirmation teacher is a heretic. Or whatever. If you want to, and even if you don't, at some point you will find a reason to be angry at your parish. Eventually you will probably find a reason to leave. The question is, should you?

The Church is organized into parishes for a reason. In fact, if you go to Louisiana the state itself is organized into parishes instead of counties. Yes, I was confused too the first time I spoke there. *Parish* is not a synonym for *church building,* but rather for the geographic territory of a given Christian community. I'm embarrassed to say that after driving in my rental car for the first time speaking in Louisiana and arriving at the church, I told the priest I was impressed with how many Catholic churches there were there. Yeah, he laughed too.

Most parishes are made up of a mix of people, some of whom live within the "territory" of the parish and some of whom do not. Why might people want to belong to a church outside their territory? Well, given how parishes are divided up, they may actually be closer to one than to the parish they technically belong to. Or maybe this parish has a school and the parish they live in doesn't. Or maybe Mom or Dad teaches at the school or works in the parish. Or maybe there's a longtime family connection to the place. Or maybe they just like the priest better. Or the music. Or the kneelers. People will choose parishes for all sorts of reasons, some of them very good and some of them very silly. But how we choose our parish is important, and how we choose to live in that parish is more important.

There is a real value to the traditional system of territorial parishes. For one thing, it ensures that we are connected to the actual places in which we live. Our fellow parishioners are, at least theoretically, those Catholics who live near us. This can help build unity even outside the confines of the parish campus or the church proper. Teresa and I have grown closer with a couple on my block because they are parishioners of the same church we are. He's the only guy who will walk to my house and let me know when my dog has escaped the yard. It also helps ensure a certain measure of diversity within the parish itself. While we've always had rich parishes and poor parishes, the Church is usually careful to draw the lines in such a way that both rich and poor people wind up in the same parish together. The parish should be at least as diverse as the neighborhood in which it operates.

Of course, there can be good reasons not to attend your local parish. If, for instance, you work nights and have to attend an early Mass on your way home and your local parish only has Mass later in the morning, then probably you are better off simply switching to the place across town that has the early morning Mass. Traditionally language was another good reason to belong to a parish outside the neighborhood in which you lived, and that still holds true today. If, say, Spanish or Vietnamese is your primary language and there is a parish that offers Mass in your native tongue nearby, then registering there as opposed to the place across the street might make more sense, even if you still make visits and sometimes hit up daily Mass at the closer church.

Many times people choose not to belong to their local parish because they don't "feel fed" there or get anything out of it. Again, I speak at missions in dozens of parishes across the country each year, and with rare exceptions, I just don't buy it. You get out of Mass precisely what you put into it. Sure, you might prefer one kind of music to another, or one style of liturgy, or one priest's preaching, but none of those are really compelling reasons to leave a parish and join another. What's more, when there is real trouble going on and all of the most influential parishioners pick up and leave, nobody is left to help rebuild. Switching parishes for political or stylistic reasons can confine us to ourselves, not challenging us to grow in charity toward each other. In fact, leaving can actually encourage the bad behavior we hope to avoid.

The point is that when there is trouble or discomfort among the faithful, we need to develop a virtuous way of dealing with it. Moving to another parish is rarely the right decision. In fact, if we constantly run away from or avoid conflicts or discomfort, then sooner or later the same kind of thing will happen in the new parish. It's not reasonable to believe that we'll never have conflict within our parish families, that Father will never make any mistakes, that every family, every other parishioner will be the nicest person we have ever met. It is reasonable to expect, though, that people centered on the words and actions of Jesus Christ will respond to the normal sorts of internal conflicts and personal difficulties in the same way he did, as an example of hope and holiness to the rest of the world.

BELONGING

It is a great privilege to belong to God's family, but also a great responsibility. It doesn't mean that we're signing up for perfection, or even that we can expect such from our fellow family members, but it does mean that we are being held to a higher standard. That's the price of belonging to God's family: We are held up to God's standards. Though we are each found wanting in our own right, it is Christ who makes it possible for people like us to make it, to attain heights we never could on our own, and to become the sort of people we never knew we could be. God gives us a place to belong permanently. And we have the great privilege of inviting other people in as well.

But make no mistake as to what you're inviting them into. Catholicism is beautiful, in all her teachings, in her ritual, in her life of faith, but it is often easier to reflect upon that in the abstract rather than in concrete, practical situations. There is a priest who is one of the holiest I know. The reverence with which he approaches the altar and his devotion to Jesus Christ in the Eucharist is like none other. But for the life of him, he has the most difficult time getting up for it in the morning. Sometimes the smartest and holiest people we know have a hard time staying awake for a particular homily, or yawn through the Eucharistic prayer. But you see, that is where holiness is found. It's in the cantor who drives us nuts because he thinks he's on Broadway, or the lady who distributes Holy Communion each Sunday as though she's greeting people at a retail store , touching your arm and all. These aren't just opportunities to put up with bad behavior or offer serious correction. They're chances for us to grow in holiness, the holiness of a family that, like all of our families, is ridiculous at times and at others very, very saintly.

PRAYER
It Does a Family Good

You've already read that the best gift you can give to your kids is to really love your spouse. That's true, and it's part of being the best spouse that you can be. And growing in that love and holiness together takes hard work and lots of time, but that's not all. Prayer is perhaps the greatest gift that we can give to our families, both in the home and outside of it. I tend to highlight more of the importance of prayer together under our roofs each day, as many of us are already praying together at Mass each week.

The kind of prayer I am talking about, however, is not just the twenty-two-second prayer that we say before meals, but prayer that takes time, involving Scripture, reflection, and private devotion. It is in bringing our immortal souls and the immortal souls of our spouses and kids to God that we find our meaning, purpose, and sanctity for our families in Jesus Christ.

I know that this sounds idealistic. I know that we're all busy, and I know that the older kids get, the more activities they get involved in, and the more entrenched we get in our careers, the harder it is to get time together just to eat dinner, let alone to sit down and pray. But Mother Teresa wasn't kidding; the family that prays together really does stay together. Not only that, a family that regularly prays together will do more than just survive intact—the practice of regular family prayer will help each member individually and the family unit as a whole thrive.

THE GAME PLAN

If you have ever been to one of my missions, then you know my basic game plan. My goal is to get you and your family praying together every single day. It doesn't have to be long—just dedicated, intentional time with the Lord and your family. I recommend seven minutes a day to start. Some people have a hard time with five. A few work themselves up to twenty minutes or even half an hour. But for the sake of getting started, whether you're a couple about to get married, a family of six with everyone still at home, or a recently retired couple married four or five decades, start small, be intentional, and let the Lord work something great in your marriages, your families, and your own spiritual lives.

Understand, I'm not telling you to sit down and "Say your prayers" for seven minutes. A lot of us were taught as children to kneel down by our beds and say a series of prayers before going to sleep: the Our Father, the Hail Mary, the Glory Be, maybe the Angel of God prayer, followed by a long list of "And God bless . . ." which typically involved everyone from Mom and Dad to Aunt Sally, as well as all the goldfish in the tank. Starting or ending your prayer time with some special intentions is a good idea, but you don't want three minutes of rattling off rote prayers and then only three minutes of real quality time with the Lord. Begin your time, put in your time, and then close your time together, and you'll see results. I promise.

THERE IS A TIME AND
A PLACE FOR EVERYTHING

Obviously time is the most precious resource most of us have. We work, go to school, clean the house, do the shopping, get meals together, exercise, run errands, visit Grandma and Grandpa, plan vacations, go to church, belong to clubs, get the kids to practice, go to their games, volunteer, help the kids with homework, and hopefully have time to work on our relationships, especially our marriages. The trouble is that it's hard enough to fit all of this into a life together, let alone lopping some other requirement onto the rest. But the point is that taking time to pray shouldn't be some sort of special event in the life of your family; it should, rather, simply be part of your daily life. In fact, it probably already is to some extent. Many of us remember to pray before meals, or at least before the main meal of the day. And we probably have taught our kids at least some of the "classic" Catholic prayers. And of course we do go to Mass on Sundays and holy days, or at least we know we should. Maybe we even take turns praying with the kids before bed. So don't look at this like it's some additional thing, but more like it's just rescheduling something that you already do together, like moving the family dinner from five to six in the evening, or making Saturday morning the time to do chores as opposed to Sunday night.

But finding a time when you have your whole family together can be a real problem, especially if you have older kids in sports or other activities. A lot of people naturally choose just before bed, or at least just before the kids go to bed, because that's the time that they're most likely to have everyone together. That's not a bad idea, and it certainly works for some people. My wife, Teresa, and I typically pray at night just before bed, but I'm often up for another hour or so after the fact. The trouble with this time is that people are usually quite tired and often have a hard time concentrating enough to really give themselves to prayer. Prayer itself is naturally relaxing and so can actually exacerbate the situation. It's a difficult thing. Obviously we should have the kind of comfort with the Lord that if we fall asleep during prayer occasionally it's not the end of the world. At the same time, if you constantly fell asleep in the middle of a serious conversation with your spouse, he or she obviously wouldn't be very happy with you. You wouldn't be taking the situation very seriously. There can also be side effects. My grandma taught her kids to all say the rosary at night in bed, especially if they were scared or couldn't sleep. That's not a bad solution, and the rosary certainly can be very soothing, but the trouble is that it forms a habit. Every time my good friend hears a Hail Mary she begins to yawn. And if there's a whole rosary ever said at a wake, she's out halfway through.

A good alternative time is just before the evening meal. Typically our meals can be "held" for five or ten minutes. Sitting at the kitchen table or in the living room can provide an atmosphere that is relaxing enough but not sleep inducing. Of course, the very smell of the food can be a distraction, so if you're having curry, you may want to pray at a different time for that day.. If your family consistently rises early enough that you're not running around crazy in the morning, then sometimes this is a good time too. I have some good friends with a little five-year-old who gets up on his own every morning at six and stumbles into his parents' room to snuggle up between them. They use their first ten minutes or so every morning to pray.

So you see, the place can vary too. It depends in large part upon the needs of your family. Sometimes everyone climbing into Mom and Dad's bed can be a great way to pray. For other families it might make everyone sleepy, ready for a movie, or possibly charged up for a pillow fight. Depending upon the furniture, the living room might be a good space, but if you have kids—or grown-ups, for that matter—who are easily distracted, that might not be a good choice. Kitchens can be a kind of neutral territory, but if there's food cooking it can be terribly distracting. Play it by ear and tend to the needs of your own family. Your prayer space may change over the years too, and that's okay. As a young couple you may always pray in bed before going to sleep. With a newborn maybe the nursery is the place to pray, especially when putting the baby to bed. Maybe a toddler or slightly older child needs some more structure and so the kitchen table or living room becomes the place. Maybe your older kids are fighting a lot in the game room and so you decide to start having prayer there to kind of reclaim the space for God and good behavior. If you live in a warm enough climate or if some seasons are particularly good, maybe a porch or deck would be a good place to pray. There are as many different possibilities as there are families and family configurations.

There are two things I would recommend universally, however. Whatever space you choose, mark it somehow—in other words, sanctify it. Put up a holy image of the Lord or Our Lady, or if the space allows for it maybe even build a little devotional altar. Teresa and I have a beautiful picture of Mary holding the baby Jesus hanging beside our bed. That has certainly been the object my eyes gaze upon during this holy time together. You may never have done this but have probably seen it in movies or on TV. Oftentimes in certain ethnic groups, but also sometimes when people die unexpectedly a little memorial develops; it typically involves a table or shelf, some kind of a covering or tablecloth, some candles, an image of two, and maybe even written prayers left in offering. There's a long tradition of devotional altars in Catholic homes, and I find that they can be very helpful for setting up a room as a sort of default prayer space or chapel. My mom and dad have one, and though they keep putting things on it (Saint Joseph and Saint Therese are getting a little crowded), it became the centerpiece for the times my family prayed together. It's not that the room can't be used for other things too, but when no one else is around it might be where we go to pray. If a permanent space isn't possible, say, you're using the kitchen table, then maybe at least bring out an icon or image and a small candle when you sit down to pray.

The other thing that I would recommend is to be consistent until this really becomes a habit. Find a time that works and stick with it, and then stick with it some more, and wait until you're on vacation, totally out of your regular routine, and together you as a family might just find yourselves gathering to pray at the regular time. That's when you know you've got it. But if you let yourselves waffle too much at the beginning, it will likely never become a true habit and you won't be doing as well by your spouse and your kids as you could be.

MUCH ADO ABOUT . . . WHAT?

Okay, so you and your family have set up a regular time to pray. You've dedicated some physical space for the purpose and are now ready to begin your daily round of seven minutes together with the Lord. But just what do you do when you get there?

The answer to that is, again, as unique as you and your family. The thing about prayer and the great lesson to be both learned and taught in this time of family prayer is that prayer is as deeply personal an activity as one can engage in. There are as many ways to pray to and relate to God as there are people to do the praying, and so just how you go about this intimate time with the Lord and your family is really up to you. One important thing to remember, however, is that in all conversations we need to both speak and listen. Too often with God we do all of the talking, which is ironic since he knows our needs ahead of time anyway. These few moments of silence with your family might be the only quiet time of your whole day. Relish them, and don't be afraid to share them with your kids.

Basically you can do this any way you want. I would recommend starting off with the sign of the cross and then naming whatever special intentions or petitions you need to remember. Then someone could simply say a brief spontaneous prayer dedicating the time to the Lord. You could choose to read a short passage from the Scriptures, possibly for the day, a novena, or some other prayer. Then everyone should do their best to sit in silence for a couple of minutes. Especially at the beginning, repeating a familiar prayer such as the Hail Mary could be helpful, or even a decade of the rosary. Then, toward the end, everyone could join in the Our Father prayerfully and slowly. The leader could say a short closing prayer and everyone end with the sign of the cross. This is much like the routine Teresa and I follow, but again, pray as your family is most comfortable praying.

There are literally hundreds of other possibilities. The tradition of the Church is simply chock-full of ways to pray, popular devotions, and special patrons. In fact, one thing that I strongly recommend is picking a patron for your family. You already have some natural patrons: your patron saint, your spouse's patron saint, the patron of whatever work you both do, the patron of the place you're from (you do have one—just check with your pastor), but one thing that I've found really effective, especially in talking to young couples preparing for marriage, is to have them choose a special patron of their relationship. This saint becomes kind of like the patron saint of their family. Maybe an icon or image of this saint is what you want to keep on that little home altar or in the center of the kitchen table. Then this saint can be invoked at the beginning and end of every prayer session. And, of course, don't forget to call upon those saints in our own lives who have gone before us in death. This certainly goes for parents and grandparents, but even for children who have been miscarried or who passed early on. Sometimes this is an especially good way both to help you through your grief and also to introduce your living children to their dead brother or sister in a helpful, healthy sort of way. Call on these people to pray for you, ask them to be present even as your family prays still, and don't be afraid to ask for very special favors from those you love best.

The key is to tailor the time to the needs, desires, gifts, and talents of those present. Maybe you or your spouse are an especially good artist. Well then, draw a picture of your patron or some other holy image and bring it to your time of prayer, even as the work is developing. Or if you're writing a poem, or even putting together a legal brief, don't be afraid to bring in the physical signs of your labor and present them before God each day. If your family is musically inclined, then perhaps some singing during your time of prayer would be a very natural thing. I know in my case it would simply send my wife running, but you never know till you try. Just put in the time, out loud or in silence, but always contemplative, connecting to God all the while.

IF AT FIRST YOU DON'T SUCCEED

The first time Teresa and I tried to pray together—really pray together, like I'm suggesting here—was a total disaster. Teresa wasn't a Catholic yet but was being a good sport about everything. I'd decided that we were going to end with a Hail Mary. Well, we voiced some intentions and spent some time together in silence, and then I started the Hail Mary. I couldn't finish it. For whatever reason, for the life of me I simply couldn't remember the prayer. So here I am, this former seminarian turned Catholic speaker trying to convince my girlfriend how important it is that we pray together, and I can't even get through the oldest prayer I know. Yep, that was awkward.

Of course, Teresa got it, and I think ultimately she was truly touched by the whole thing. Praying together is very intimate, and letting her see that very weak, very confused, very nervous part of me was a major turning point in our relationship. And even my frustration with myself just showed her a) how important my faith is to me, b) how important devotion to Our Lady is to me, and c) why it was important for me to share all of this with her. And now we do share it—all of it—and when I forget my prayers, she helps me to finish them.

I have a priest friend who when he prepares couples for marriage asks them a number of questions. In the course of the conversation he'll ask if the couple has been sexually intimate. Of course, these days the answer is yes more often than not. Then, later on in the conversation he'll ask if they pray together. They typically get a little bit sheepish and one or the other will point out that they say grace before meals. Father will point out that grace before meals is great, and that they do pray more than they think because they come to Mass at least sometimes or he wouldn't be seeing them there, but then he'll simply observe, "Why is it so much easier to sleep with somebody than to pray with them?" Besides living in a very sexually permissive culture, this does highlight something important that you'll need to be aware of before you even try to begin this practice, especially if you are a couple either recently married or preparing for marriage. Just like sex, prayer produces intimacy. It's why so often we teach our kids to pray in their rooms right before bed—because that is as quiet, safe, and intimate a place as they have in their lives just yet. And it will establish new bonds of intimacy even in the midst of already good, holy, healthy relationships.

I want you to try hard at this, and I want it in some ways to be difficult—but not too difficult—and I want you to persevere and find the blessings of prayer with your family. But make no mistake, there are no real external criteria here for success. There's no magic number of specifically desired outcomes to be attained. You can't get gold stars for praying well any more than you can get them for being a good mom or dad or spouse. It's just about the relationship—the relationship you have with God and that your whole family shares with God. When one of you suffers or struggles, so do all of the members, but when one of you succeeds and finds delight in the Lord, so too will all of you. So if it's tough at first to stay faithful or undistracted, or to get everyone there and together and happy (which can be as difficult as anything else), keep trying. Eventually it will work, not because you've passed some milestone or won some award, but because one day you will wake up and realize that just doing what you're doing is what you were meant to be up to all along.

BUT MY FAMILY . . .

Besides the normal objections—we don't have time; my kids can't sit still; I can't sit still; it's too hard; I'm not sure it's worth it—some people will worry that their families are too dysfunctional or too unconventional to try something like this. It may well be that some special circumstance prevents all or part of your family from participating in regular family prayer, either some of the time or all of the time. In my experience, though, it often happens less than you think.

One worry is often that a family is blended. That is, maybe you live with your spouse and her kids, and you are only their stepdad. Their birth father might have them on the weekends, or holidays, or there might be some other arrangement. The expectations surrounding family prayer should be handled in the same way all other family obligations are handled whenever the kids are at your house. If eating the evening meal together is a general expectation and it gets missed only in very rare circumstances, then so should prayer be. It doesn't matter if they don't pray at their other parent's home or if the other parent prays with them very differently. At your house you are responsible for them. Use your own best judgment.

Other people worry about other adults in the house. Certainly if you have parents or grandparents living with you then they should not only be invited to participate in the family prayer, but you should do your best to make them feel welcome. If you're a newly married couple and you're living with your folks or your spouse's and you want to pray in bed a lot, then obviously that might not be the place you want to pray as a family. But if you and your husband are raising your kids and it becomes necessary to move one or both of your parents in with you, then inviting them to participate in the family prayer at least some of the time is important. The same might go for guests, be they long or short term. While you want to be respectful of your children's friends if they happen to be over, either at dinnertime or for a sleepover, if family prayer falls in the middle of it, you might consider bringing them in on it.

One special circumstance is what to do if members of the family are from a different faith tradition, or maybe have no faith at all. The Church is and wants to be extremely respectful of the authentic beliefs of other people. As such, we should never force people to pray in a way that makes them feel uncomfortable or like they have to say something they don't believe in. At the same time, our praying one way and inviting others to join us in the prayer doesn't mean that we expect them to participate wholesale. Just make sure that the ground rules are clear from the outset. If your brother's kid comes to stay for a week and your brother is a Pentecostal, make sure that you don't force the kid to say the rosary. That will only cause problems between you and your brother and will likely make it harder to win him back. At the same time, exposing your nephew to your nightly family prayer, in which he is invited to voice his intentions and sit in silence with you, and you later say a decade of the rosary, may wind up being the spark that lights the fire to bring them to life in the Church. There may be times when it is best just not to do family prayer because of the presence of too many outsiders from too many diverse backgrounds to keep straight and be respectful of, but seriously, this happens way, way less than you would think. Frankly, most people will just be impressed that you and your family strive to pray every day.

WHAT ABOUT ME?

What if you don't have any family? What if your spouse is gone, your kids have grown up, and nowadays you're living alone? How can you engage in family prayer? What does my work or my mission have to do with you? Everything. And you'll see how.

Widows and widowers have long had a special place in the Church. In fact, widows used to be regarded almost like religious sisters and nuns are today. They have much to teach us about relationships and life. My grandmothers, for instance, by their wisdom and example helped me to better understand the virtue of love, despite loss, giving me an example to look too in my marriage. These men and woman are also some of the most powerful intercessors of prayer I know, praying for my family at home, our families in the parish, and our Catholic family abroad.

Even if you're single and divorced, or if someone else has custody of your kids, or if you are an adult living alone with an aging parent, the principles of daily family prayer apply directly to your life, and the role of intercessor falls in a very special way to you. Very, very few of us have no relationship to any family. As parents, grandparents, aunts or uncles, cousins, close family friends, and especially godparents or confirmation sponsors, we have a special obligation to pray for those in our charge. Daily prayer needs to form part of the life of every single Christian. If we are living on our own for whatever reason, then we have an obligation to pray for those to whom we are related by blood or affection, and for whom we have assumed care, especially in the Church. The lives we live, lives of work and play and family life, grounded in and supported by daily prayer, make possible the lives that our friends, neighbors, children, and godchildren are able to live in Christ, whether we ever see the fruits of our labor or not. Whether our family lives close by or far away, our prayers are powerful, necessary, and profoundly important.

Of course, those who live alone also have a special sort of obligation to find other Christians to pray with. Daily Mass is a wonderful opportunity that too few of us take advantage of regularly. Adoration of the Blessed Sacrament is another good practice. Just imagine the effect you might have on your grandkids if on a day at the zoo or the amusement park you stop by the adoration chapel for ten minutes on your way there to ask God's blessings on the day, or on the way home to thank him for all the fun. Finally, just having good Christian friends you can relate to and pray with even semi-regularly is an essential component of the single Christian's life.

SHAPE THE CIRCLE EVER WIDER

We all have special people in our lives, those to whom we owe a great deal and those we have to take care of. If we're married, our first obligation is to our spouse and our kids. We have to do our best to live a life of faith and good practice in the Church. We have to pass on the faith to them and allow them to continue to help convert us. We have to take advantage of things like Catholic schools, CCD programs, and other religious education opportunities, not only to prepare our kids for the sacraments, but to help them grow into lives of faith. And we have to be a regular part of the faithful by consistently attending Mass, observing important feast days, and doing everything we can to follow the moral teachings of our Catholic faith.

Of course, our circle of influence and obligation is way bigger than the four walls of our house. We have an obligation to our kids and grandkids, to our nieces and nephews, aunts and uncles, parents and friends, and especially to those with whom we have a special bond in the faith. The vows you took as a godparent or confirmation sponsor were just as serious as the vows you took the day you were married. At a bare minimum you need to pray for your godchildren and confirmandi, but you also need to keep in touch with them, pray with them, and if they stray gently call them back. And we have similar obligations just by being part of a regular parish. If you teach religious education, then your students and their families are part of your own life of faith. If you're a teacher or an administrator at a Catholic school, then your circle of influence is very big. Even if you're a single person who always sits in the same pew, every Sunday you have people who are part of your family—hopefully with the same mission as yours—sitting right next to you and across from you and behind you at Mass. You may not know their names, but they are a part of you, and so you are a part of them. Tend to them well, because God has given them to you.

But our care for the Church and the wider world starts at home. So the regular practice of daily prayer, even for just seven minutes a day, will literally change the whole tenor of your spiritual life. If your prayer life is already good, it will make it better. If your family life is already strong, it will make it stronger. If your charity is genuine, it will make you more loving, and your kids and your families and all of those you meet. If you start praying regularly as a family, then it won't matter so much what you say; you'll be sharing the faith by the very way you live your life.

SACRAMENTS

We all have people who are clearly part of our families but who are not related to us by blood. Whether it's the old lady up the street whom our family "adopted," the ex-in-law who never seems to go away, or just a good friend of a cousin who has been around so long nobody knows the difference anymore, what makes a person a part of the family has a lot less to do with blood relation and a lot more to do with a shared life; common hopes, dreams, values, and ideals; and especially a common commitment to each other. God's family, the Church, is made up of people like this. We obviously hope our relatives are also part of the Church, but relationships in the Church itself are based upon something much more profound. In the Church, God's family is defined by a common faith, common worship, and common service. Everyone knows how crucial sacraments are to the life of Catholics. In fact, most catechesis and Catholic school education programs are designed in some way around sacramental preparation. The reason for this is that the sacraments are the ordinary situations, experiences, and encounters in which we meet God. From the outside they can simply appear to be empty rituals or bare symbols. Yes, they are symbols and they are rituals, but they are much more than that. Sacraments are sacred symbols, holy signs that actually communicate what they represent. This is obviously the hardest thing for most people to believe about the sacraments, but it is also the most important. Once you've got a sacramental vision, once you get that God actually does stuff with stuff—the regular, old, everyday stuff of real life—then all of that regular, old, everyday stuff becomes an opportunity to encounter the living God.

Sometimes sacraments get confused with special events or particular milestones in a person's life. It's true that the sacraments parallel many of the important moments in our natural lives. The first major event in most of our lives is our birth, and so the first major event of life in the Spirit is baptism, which is a kind of rebirth. In this country we usually give confirmation around the time a person begins to take on at least some adult responsibility in the world, and so in practice it becomes a kind of Christian bar mitzvah marking one's "adulthood in the Church." Marriage and Holy Orders mark a transition into a committed stage of adult life. The anointing of the sick has long been associated with end-of-life issues and so gets paired with death as a kind of "last sacrament." Of course, some of these connections are real, but others are a bit of a stretch. Baptism is designed to be a kind of rebirth, which is the reason even Jesus talks about it that way. Marriage and ordination are about commitment, but they can happen at various times in a person's life. But while confirmation often happens at fourteen or sixteen or eighteen, it also happens to children as young as seven, or sometimes even to infants. More important, the two sacraments we should all be receiving most frequently, penance and Holy Communion, don't precisely parallel a time or event in life, but are more like the regular patterns of life. Sin and failure are part of most people's daily lives, as is eating. The point of the sacraments is not just to mark certain moments but to sanctify all of our lives, so that eating and drinking and living and working and everything in between become moments of

70

authentic encounter with the living God. That's why the "special events" model is incomplete, and can at times even confuse or obscure the actual meaning of the sacrament.

The sacraments can be organized in any number of ways, but since Vatican II one way has become much more common than the others. We'll take our lead from the council and look first at the sacraments of Christian initiation, namely baptism, confirmation/chrismation, and Eucharist. Next we'll look at the sacraments of healing, which help us to live our daily lives as Christians, namely anointing and penance. Finally, we'll look at the two sacraments of vocation: matrimony and Holy Orders. We'll also touch on the vocation to religious life and see why, among other things, Orders is a sacrament but religious life is not.

BAPTISM

Most of us don't remember our baptism. This is because we are typically baptized as infants. The symbolism is pretty clear when you have a newborn being "born again" of water and the Holy Spirit within days or weeks of her natural birth. At the same time because few of us can remember our own baptism we mostly experience this sacrament by way of somebody else's. It can be hard, at times, to see the significance of dressing a little baby up in a white robe and dribbling a few drops of water on her forehead. But this is the most important day of her young life, whether she can ever remember it or not. The *Catechism of the Catholic Church*, quoting Saint Gregory, puts it this way:

> Baptism is God's most beautiful and magnificent gift. . . .
> We call it gift, grace, anointing, enlightenment, garment
> of immortality, bath of rebirth, seal, and most precious

gift. It is called gift because it is conferred on those who bring nothing of their own; grace since it is given even to the guilty; Baptism because sin is buried in the water; anointing for it is priestly and royal as are those who are anointed; enlightenment because it radiates light; clothing since it veils our shame; bath because it washes; and seal as it is our guard and the sign of God's Lordship. (CCC 1216)

As I said, I don't remember my baptism, but I've certainly heard a lot about it. I know where it happened, who my godparents are, who the priest was, and most of all, I know that there was a party afterward. Now, in our own human way we can let this get away from us sometimes; i.e. when a second-grade mother makes a bigger deal out of the first Communion party than the Communion itself, but the instinct is absolutely right. Every sacrament should be accompanied by some kind of a celebration. That's why sacraments are typically celebrated during Mass, which is itself a way that God throws us a party.

The point is that baptism changes absolutely everything. This is hard enough to see when the person being baptized is a tiny baby, let alone when the person is an adult. For this reason, and for some others, the Church makes the ceremony around adult baptism a little bit bigger than with kids, not because they're better or more important, but because the memories will last for the grown-up in a way that they won't for the child.

The greatest moment in the whole Church year is the solemn vigil of Easter. As best as we can tell, from the very beginning Christians gathered on the Saturday preceding Easter Sunday to await the anniversary of the Lord's resurrection from the dead. Three symbols came to dominate: light and darkness, water, and Eucharist.

The Church now as then gathers in the darkness. Then the great fire is lit, the new Easter fire, which is passed on to the greatest candle in the Church. From this candle smaller tapers are lit by all the members of the Church. The deacon proclaims, "Christ, our light!" And the people respond, "Thanks be to God!" Christ, the light who has burned from before the foundation of the world, enters into the darkness of the church building, pierces the cold darkness of the tomb, and brings new and lasting light.

After the readings have been read and the gospel proclaimed and preached it is time to initiate the new Christians. As I said earlier, Teresa entered the Church just before we were married, and so we were able to experience this in an intimate way. These new Christians have been prepared over a long period of time, often more than a year, and in the weeks preceding have publicly proclaimed their intention to enter the Church. First they are called by name, even as each of us is called by God. Each and every one of us is called by name by God. In the ancient world this often meant literally taking a brand-new name, a name that belonged to a Christian who was already dead, and probably murdered for the faith. Being called by name establishes a new relationship between us and God and gives us a clue of just how close God is to us in all of this.

Next those to be baptized are asked to make a series of promises or vows. These don't look like ordinary vows, however. They are basically a commitment to avoid sin and evil and to do good, followed by a profession of faith. That's why saying the Creed at Mass each Sunday is so important. It's renewing our baptismal promises. Now, of course, those of us baptized as infants didn't make the promises for ourselves; our parents and godparents made them for us. This is why godparents are meant by the Church to be such important characters in the Christian's life.

73

They make promises on your behalf as Christians, and then are responsible to see that you can follow through on what they have promised. So when you're picking out godparents for your kids, don't simply imagine the honor your buddy will feel when you ask him to be godfather to your firstborn; make sure he actually goes to Mass, believes what the Church says, and is a man of his word who will follow through on what he says before God and everyone else.

Sometimes when adults are baptized they are asked to lie down on the ground in a gesture we call "prostration." The gesture is required at things like religious profession and ordination, but it makes sense at a baptism because when else is a person's whole life going to be more perfectly "handed over" to Christ Jesus? While they are prostrate the Church prays the litany of the saints, especially invoking the patron saints of the people to be baptized (i.e. their Christian names), asking the saints to intercede for them and protect them.

Finally, they are taken to the water. In ancient churches the font was often a deep pool, and those to be baptized would walk down into it and then walk up again. The font becomes then both womb and tomb. From the womb of the Church new Christians are born. From the tomb of the dead, the now-living Christ raises his friends to new life.

If you haven't gotten it yet, baptism is chock-full of symbolism. The newly baptized are given fresh, clean clothes, which are as white as possible to symbolize the purity they now have in Christ. They are then given candles lit from the great Easter candle, which was lit at the start of the service. This light is entrusted to them until the day of the Lord's coming. When the person being baptized is an infant, the candle, and so the newborn's faith, is entrusted to the parents and godparents, "to be kept burning brightly."

74

Baptism is how the Church, or rather God through the Church, makes new Christians. Like all sacraments, it makes present what it signifies. The washing with the water signifies a cleansing of sin, and baptism absolutely and unchangeably washes away sins. Those of us who are baptized when we are older are forgiven all of our sins at the moment of our baptism, which is why even people who have persecuted the Church (like Saint Paul) can, after baptism, become great saints. But baptism is also about being buried in the tomb with Christ and rising to new life with him, and so the "old man" of sin and weakness is buried in the tomb while the "new man" rises with Christ. Ancient baptismal fonts were often even shaped like tombs.

Ultimately, though, baptism is about conversion and intention and entrance into a community of believers. It is not about perfection but the desire to be perfect. It is not about an individual decision but about a community's willingness to take on a new person. It is not about putting an end to difficulty and suffering, but about putting difficulty and suffering to good use.

CONFIRMATION

While most of us don't remember our baptisms, we can probably remember very well our confirmations. Typically this happens sometime between the ages of seven and eighteen, though in some places it might even be given to infants. This is because confirmation is not about our confirming our faith, but about God confirming something in us. If we're old enough when it happens, then we have to agree to receive that grace, just as we couldn't force-feed someone Holy Communion, but the grace of the sacrament doesn't depend upon some sense of our "readiness" to receive it.

Confirmation leaves an indelible mark on the soul of the confirmed. So does baptism. So, for that matter, does ordination. Practically speaking, this just means that one cannot be confirmed twice, or baptized twice, or ordained twice (to the same position). Spiritually, though, this is quite significant. The work that is done in the sacrament is so unique that it cannot be repeated. This is obviously not the work of the adolescent or young adult who musters up enough faith to want to be a good Christian for the rest of her life. That is good and necessary, but we all know that her work can be revoked, at least on its own. What God does is empower that choice and enlighten that faith. He confirms the work already begun in baptism and leads it closer to its inevitable conclusion: life with him forever in heaven.

When the Church celebrates confirmation, the bishop or priest conferring the sacrament will lay hands on the candidates, either individually or as a group, and pray a very long and special prayer. This is because the Church sees the roots of confirmation in the laying on of hands that the apostles performed in the early Church on the newly baptized. The prayer is all about the Holy Spirit, who comes with the sevenfold gifts announced by the prophet Isaiah and repeated by Christ in the Gospels: wisdom, understanding, counsel, fortitude, knowledge, piety, and reverence. These gifts are the basic traits that should characterize the life of an "enspirited" Catholic. This is then sealed or finished by the anointing with oil and the words "Be sealed with the gifts of the Holy Spirit." With these words the person being confirmed is set apart for something sacred. Bishops and priests are anointed with oil and set apart for something sacred too, but while what they are set apart for is primarily something in the Church, confirmation sets apart all Christians for something sacred in the world. That is, at its heart, the essence of evangelization.

The oil used for confirmation is very special. It is called the Sacred Chrism and is made and blessed only once a year by the bishop at a special Mass called the Chrism Mass. Because of this, in the Eastern churches this sacrament is called "chrismation." In some parts of the Church we also call baptisms "christenings." Both are essentially the same word; they are both related to Christ. The word christ, in Greek, means "anointed." Those who have been chrismated have been anointed. Those who have been christened have been "Christed" or turned into little Christs. Together, baptism and confirmation work to do just that.

EUCHARIST

As Saint John Vianney said, "If man understood the mystery of the Mass, he would die of love." This is a great reminder for us as we reflect on the gift of the Eucharist. When we think of the Eucharist as sacrament we are probably tempted to think of first Communion, but of course every time we receive Holy Communion we are receiving a sacrament. The parties and gifts that most of us remember from first Holy Communion are important, however, because they remind us of the kind of joy we should have every single time we receive.

Eucharist or Holy Communion completes Christian initiation. All of the work of baptism and confirmation leads one ultimately to the altar. By baptism one is grafted or sewn onto the body of Christ, the Church. In confirmation one is strengthened by the Holy Spirit to act as a "little Christ" in the world and keep faithful to the commitments of baptism. In Holy Communion it is Christ himself who enters us, to give us strength, to sustain us, and to prepare us for what lies ahead. Holy Communion sustains us here on earth and gives us a foretaste of heaven. It connects us

77

to everything that's gone before and everything that will come again. Holy Communion makes present the reality it signifies in the most perfect way, because while all of the sacraments aim to make the grace of Christ present under some particular circumstance, it is only in Communion that Christ himself is both present and received.

The Holy Eucharist is the greatest of sacraments, and those who participate in it cannot help but be changed. It is the sacrament most readily available, and yet most frequently neglected. It is perhaps the simplest looking—the bare remnants of a simple meal—but in it are the whole of heaven and earth, all the good of the created world and whole presence of the Uncreated One. The fullness of participation in the Holy Mass involves Holy Communion, but those received to Eucharist at the Easter vigil are privileged first to even be there, for if they were just baptized then, at least theoretically, they've never even been present for the whole Mass before. In the ancient world this was absolute. Nobody who wasn't a baptized and confirmed Christian was even permitted to stay for the liturgy of the Eucharist. In the Russian Church the deacon still has a line just before the Creed is recited: "The doors! The doors!" This is an ancient sign to bar the doors from those not already initiated into the Christian community because of the holy mystery about to be celebrated.

This is also why our liturgies are so beautiful. The story is told that Vladimir the Great, an ancient emperor of Russia, wanted to unite his kingdom with one religion. He sent representatives out across both Europe and Asia, all of the known world, to observe every major religious tradition. Those who came back from a Christian Eucharist in Constantinople were astounded. "We knew not whether we were in Heaven or on Earth. . . . We only know that God dwells there among the people!"

Every Mass is a meeting of heaven and earth. This is why the Eucharist is called the "source and summit of the Christian life." It is the source because in the Eucharist is Christ himself, whole and entire. It is the summit because it is the highest point of spiritual experience possible for us here on earth, and ultimately the goal that we're all striving for. The Eucharist is the source of all grace and so of all virtue and the good works of the Church. It is also the goal of the Christian life, for in the Eucharist God dwells among his people, and his people with him.

At the same time, it's no accident that Jesus chose to give us this great gift in the context of a family meal. The Passover supper, which is where Jesus celebrated the first Eucharist, was something like a cross between Thanksgiving dinner and Easter Mass. There were hymns and readings, so it was a little more formal even than our most formal meals are, but it was also definitely a meal, with real food eaten at a real table. This means that the Eucharist should be at once sublime and familiar, normal and extraordinary.

For us and our families, regular participation in the Eucharist should look like regular participation in the family meal. It should happen at a minimum weekly, and we should be especially attentive to feasts and holy days. As with our regular family meals, sometimes the company is good, and sometimes it's just kind of . . . blah. But just as you wouldn't quit going to your family's meal just because some people are cranky or boring, we can't quit going to Mass because the music is bad, the homily boring, or the priest said something unkind seventeen and a half years ago. We come to eat, and so we should come hungry and ready to do so.

One of the most profound prayers of the whole Mass comes just before we receive Holy Communion. "Lord, I am not worthy that you should enter under my roof, but only say the word and my soul shall be healed." These are the words of the centurion in Saint Matthew's Gospel. They also contain what should be the whole of our attitude, both collectively and individually, to the Eucharist. First of all, we are not worthy. It is good and extremely important to prepare for Holy Communion by going to confession, but even if you went to confession just before Mass, chances are you had at least one uncharitable thought between the moment you left the box and the moment you received the Lord. You're not worthy. I'm not worthy. Nobody is worthy. That's the whole point. Communion is a mercy of God given to the Church—for what? For healing. "Only say the word," we pray, "and my soul shall be healed." Of course, the soul runs the body, so the healing of the soul can do great things for the body too. The Eucharist is the best medicine for what ails us and the greatest strength we can receive. One of the best gifts we can give to our kids is the example of frequent and devout Communion, which we prepare for by the sacrament of reconciliation, some kind of fasting, and being especially attentive to the needs of our neighbor.

The point is that the power and splendor and glory of what happens at each Mass should knock us off our feet every time. In fact, numerous saints have been known to levitate during Mass for just this reason. Saint John of Cupertino used to fly around so much that he's the patron of aviators and pilots. All of our hearts should be so lifted from each and every Mass, even under less than ideal conditions or when a Mass is said badly.

Remember that prayer that I mentioned in an earlier chapter? The one about the priest giving his all at each and every Mass? Well, the same should be true for us. Maybe our own preparation each time we come should be:

Servant of God,

Pray at this Mass

as if it were your first Mass,

as if it were your last Mass,

as if it were your only Mass.

PENANCE

Some of my favorite stories about the saints have to do with con-fession. John Vianney used to spend hours a day in the confes-sional. People would come from all over to hear him preach and get his advice. Often enough, if he knew that the person was scared and needed support he would even offer to do the penance that he gave the person in the sacrament himself as well. Padre Pio did many of the same things, though he wasn't afraid to kick people out of the confessional if he thought they didn't mean it, or if they were trying to use the sacrament to justify bad behavior. Probably my favorite advice, however, comes from Saint Philip Neri. He always advised having a snack after going to confession. Why? Because we need to celebrate the fact of our forgiveness. Why a snack, then, instead of a whole meal? For most of us our confessions involve mostly little daily faults. He would pray that there was never need to have a feast following the penance!

The sacrament of healing that we most frequently receive has many names: confession, conversion, contrition, forgiveness, absolution, and reconciliation. No one of these concepts encom-passes the idea completely, but they all reveal something impor-tant about what happens. In the sacrament we do *confess* our sins. We strive to *convert* our hearts and turn new again to the Lord. We show our *contrition* or sorrow for our sin and ask for God's *forgiveness*. We hear the words of *absolution* by the priest and so know the healing God brings by reconciling us to himself and to the whole Church.

Confession is, in some ways, probably the hardest sacrament. Next to Holy Communion it is also probably the most readily available. Certainly the Church's idea is that we would receive it and Holy Communion the most, but most of us don't like to do it. Why? Well, first, because none of us like to admit that we've been wrong. We don't like copping to our own mistakes, and we like even less having to do it to a third party who was probably not involved in the situation at all. Most of us are convinced that given our relationship with God we can simply pray for forgiveness and he can grant it, and so if we go to confession at all it is usually during one of those large penance services they offer during Lent and Advent. "There are always a bunch of priests, so I can find one I don't know." "There are a whole lot of people, so I know that he can't spend very much time on me." You know how it goes. I have been there too. The problem with this is that the whole experience gets cheapened, becoming all about me, rather than about God and his forgiveness.

Penance services are great, but the Church doesn't offer them all the time, for a couple of reasons. First, they are pretty impractical. More important, though, most of us need to go to confession more than once or twice a year. It's true that the Church's law obliges us to go to confession only when we are conscious of mortal sin, and it's also true that most of us are probably not out committing mortal sins all the time, but most of us do struggle with something much harder to get rid of: habitual sin. The most frustrating thing for me is to walk into the confessional and confess the same things over and over and over again. And yet I can tell you from experience that it is precisely because of my going in again and again, week after week, month after month, that I've been able to get over some of the faults that held me back for years.

The Church also teaches that we shouldn't be receiving Holy Communion if we are conscious of mortal sin, and with good reason. But that doesn't mean that we go to confession before going to Mass in order to "get worthy." If we did, we certainly wouldn't pray just before Communion that we're not worthy. Rather, we reconcile our sins with God to prepare ourselves, so that we can be in the best space spiritually and psychologically to receive the graces that God longs to give us in the sacrament, and to be forgiven more deeply and transformed more profoundly into the men and women God so wants us to be.

Take your kids to reconciliation and make sure that they see you going as well. Where I live, in Des Moines, they offer confessions every Wednesday during the lunch hour at the cathedral downtown. It's always very busy, and one of the coolest things to see is the young couples, often with kids too young to go themselves. Two young professionals, or a young professional and a stay-at-home parent will meet up just to go to confession at the same time. And you know that while the one is in the box and the other is out they're praying for each other. Kids notice this stuff, and it makes a real impression. As the kids get old enough, take them too. Once a week is a pretty big commitment, but once a month ought to be something all of us can make, at least some of the time. Try it and see how much it affects you, how it changes the way you live, and how you even ask for forgiveness and reconcile with each other better in your own homes.

ANOINTING OF THE SICK

Probably the sacrament least understood and least frequently received, at least of those sacraments that can be repeated, is holy anointing or the anointing of the sick. This is a very simple sacrament that involves some quiet prayer, a laying on of hands by the priest, and anointing with holy oil. The sacrament is intended to bring healing, of both body and soul, and to bring the ill person into greater unity with Christ and the Church by uniting her suffering to his and to that of the whole world.

Until quite recently the sacrament was typically known as "extreme unction" or "last rites." This was because for most of history if you got seriously sick you simply were near death. Obviously improvements in medicine have changed that picture somewhat, so the Church has had to remind people that the sacrament is called "anointing of the sick" and not "anointing of the dying" for a reason. The purpose of the sacrament is to help people get better in both body and soul. Sometimes the body can't recover, but the real work of healing is always done in the soul. This is why it is such a mistake to wait until the very end to call the priest. It actually gives you less time to heal spiritually and prepare yourself, either for recovery or for death.

One thing that often confuses people who have never seen an anointing before is that most of the prayers are about forgiveness. In fact, it can even look a little like the sacrament of penance but without confession or absolution. This isn't because the Church believes that a person gets sick because of their sins, at least most of the time (obviously certain behaviors can result in bad physical effects: excessive smoking, drinking, use of illegal drugs, and such). But the Church prays this way because sickness and death in general are not part of God's original plan for the world.

That's important, because just as Jesus brings forgiveness of sins, he also brings healing to our bodies as well as to our souls. Look to the Gospels: Whenever he heals people from physical ailments he says, "Your sins are forgiven you." This isn't because the person's sin caused his ailment, but because illness, injury, and death are a kind of living icon of sin. A body racked by pain and sickness is what a soul looks like plagued by sin. And so the forgiveness of sin also brings about the healing of the body.

The message of the Gospel on suffering is clear. Jesus's suffering brings life, and we who are part of Jesus can bring life by our suffering too. The seemingly hopeless situation that most of us know when we suffer is a lie, and the sacrament of anointing rejects it outright. By anointing the sick person with oil we set her apart for something sacred, and her illness and even her death is a sign to the rest of us of the hope that lies in store for us because of the Gospel. That sick person becomes again for us "another Christ." Be attentive to the sick in your parish. Assist by bringing food or Holy Communion as you are able. And introduce your kids to the sacrament of anointing as early on as you can. If Grandma or Grandpa goes to the hospital and is getting anointed, try to have the kids there. If you are having surgery, even if it's not a life-or-death situation, ask the priest to anoint you after Mass on Sunday. But show your kids, and yourselves, the value of suffering and freedom that life in the Gospel brings. We evangelize, both within our families and without, first by what we do, and only afterward by what we say.

MARRIAGE

Marriage and Holy Orders are clearly the two sacraments that people most associate with adulthood, life commitment, and service to others. In some ways this last bit seems most appropriate for priests. After all, aren't they the professional religious people? Isn't service and evangelization just part and parcel of what it means for them to do their "job"? It is, as we'll see next, but first, consider marriage from the perspective of evangelization. Think back to the beginning of your marriage or your parents' marriage. What would you say was the "mission" of the marriage?

Probably one of the pieces of Scripture that gets people most riled up today is from Saint Paul's letter to the Ephesians. You know the one: "Wives, be subordinate to your husbands . . ." But I like to point out that it's only part of the passage. Here's the whole thing: *Be subordinate to one another out of reverence for Christ. Wives should be subordinate to their husbands as to the Lord. For the husband is head of his wife just as Christ is head of the church, he himself the savior of the body. As the church is subordinate to Christ, so wives should be subordinate to their husbands in everything. Husbands, love your wives, even as Christ loved the church and handed himself over for her to sanctify her, cleansing her by the bath of water with the word, that he might present to himself the church in splendor, without spot or wrinkle or any such thing, that she might be holy and without blemish. So [also] husbands should love their wives as their own bodies. He who loves his wife loves himself.* (Ephesians 5:22–29)

So you see, it's actually the husbands who get the more raw deal here. Both spouses are supposed to be subordinate to one another, but husbands are to love their wives as Christ has loved the Church. Remember how much Christ loved the Church? Yep, that's right, he died for her. That's how husbands are to love their wives. I get told that I am harder on the guys than on the gals when I speak. I guess that's just because I see myself in the men I am speaking to. I need to be reminded quite often, most of the time in a very straightforward way, to better lay down my life for Teresa. Of course, wives are to give themselves over for their husbands' sake also. Our marriages are the primary place where we live out Christ's call for sacrificial love. That's what marriage is for—a place to grow in love and in holiness. And holiness is attained in total submission of man and woman to God.

People get married for a variety of reasons, some good and some not so good. But most people who bother to go through the whole process of preparation to get married in the Church will at least say that, generally, they're getting married because they love each other. Of course, we all love lots of people we're not married to, so that begs the question: What makes marriage different? Why does my love for this person demand a permanent and exclusive bond?

Human beings are both social and sexual in nature. Therefore all of our relationships with other human beings have both a social and a sexual component. This might sound odd at first— I mean, obviously my relationship with my grandmother isn't sexual, is it? It certainly doesn't mean the tension of sexual attraction is part of every relationship, but because each of us is a man or a woman, we relate to all other people precisely as male or female, man or woman. This social-sexual dynamic is at the heart of every marriage. People will talk about striving to be, and very often are, "best friends" with their spouses. At the same time our spouse is to be our sole and unique sexual partner. When a marriage is working properly, then, we are at our most human, our most social, our most sexual, our most vulnerable when we are with our spouses.

The nature of romantic love, of sexual dynamics, and of Christian marriage is exclusivity. This goes back to the beginning, with Adam and Eve, "for this is the reason that a man leaves his father and mother and clings to his wife." The exclusive nature of such love is actually made most clear in the Incarnation. Jesus comes for all people, all times, and all places, but he does so in a particular time and place and nation. Jesus is a Jew. He will never be Irish or Italian or Native American. Jesus had a family, a mom and a stepdad and a host of other relatives. Only a few thousand people were privileged to know him in his lifetime, and fewer still were able to know him well and personally. And yet by being born in a particular place into a particular family as a member of a particular nation Jesus sanctified all nations, all peoples, all times, and all places. Married love is like that. I don't love other people less because I love my wife first and most. If my marriage is good and healthy, then the love that I have for my wife, which I should have only for my wife, should actually open me up to better love everybody else.

The great temptation is to view marriage and romantic love simply from the perspective of the wider culture, which has many good things to say about love but many unhelpful things to say as well. First of all, it does matter whom you love and how you love him or her. You ought to love your spouse differently than you love your other friends, and there should be a kind of priority list of loves in your life. But if you love well those closest to you, then you will find yourself loving others well too. Your love for your spouse and your kids should make you more conscientious about loving other people. You should find yourself being kinder to the poor, for instance, whether your kids are with you or not, because you want to be the kind of father you are teaching them to be.

You should also be paying close attention to your religious obligations, not because you have to, but because you want to. Maybe you're already good at making sure you attend Mass when on vacation as a family, but what if you're on a business trip by yourself? Maybe the family computer in the living room has a filter on it so that the kids can't easily stumble into inappropriate material, but what about the laptop that you use for work? You might not think of these at first as part of your marriage, let alone as part of the sacramental part of your marriage, but that's the thing with sacraments—they're bathed throughout with grace and goodness, even where you least expect it.

Christians do get married for love, but this love is more than affection or emotion—it is the same sort of radical self-gift that Christ offered on the cross. This love literally acquires a life of its own, which can be seen symbolically in the conception and birth of children. Day by day as the couple struggles together to grow in faith, hope, and love, they and their families become the true missionaries to the culture. This is why the work of the Church belongs not just primarily to the priests, deacons, religious, or even the parish staff, but to you, your spouse, and your family.

HOLY ORDERS

During my early years in seminary one of the priests would always forget his breviary (the little book with all the prayers that priests are supposed to pray each day), and then he'd say as he came back to get it, "I almost forgot my wife." I thought it was kind of weird at the time, but as I discerned further I began to understand what he meant. It obviously wasn't that the book was his wife or that the prayers were his wife. It was, rather, that the relationship that he had to the Church was like that of a husband to his wife. The prayers of intercession that he promised to pray each day were part of how he cared for his spouse, and the pastoral care he gave to each of us was part of how he took care of his family.

Our priests can't get married, but you can't understand Holy Orders without first understanding marriage. Marriage is about selfless love, about giving one's self up for the other, about literally handing your body over for the one you love. Priesthood is the same. The priest literally gives his body over to the Lord, which is why the Lord can speak through the priest and say things like, "This is my body. This is my blood," and "I absolve you of your sins." Our priests might not be married, but they definitely have spouses. They may not have kids of their own, but they wind up "Father" to many more than we who are married do.

Holy Orders is a badly misunderstood sacrament today. The point is not that priests have a special job in the Church or get to make special decisions; the point is, rather, that priests have a special role in the Church, and that role is to lay down their lives for us. The authority for which the Church speaks in regard to the sacramental priesthood is not its own, but the authority of Jesus Christ himself.

Priests also do not serve alone. Most parishes today have at least some assistance by a permanent deacon, and even before we started ordaining men to the diaconate permanently again in the 1970s most parishes would at least occasionally have extra priests come in to assist. And of course the bishop is part of the priest's life too, not simply because he gives the priest his assignments but also because he visits the parish for confirmations, supplies the holy oils to be used in the sacraments, and is a spiritual father to the priest, who is in turn a spiritual father to his people. This is because from the very beginning the Church has understood ordained ministry to exist in three grades or stages: deacon, priest, and bishop.

Priests are the normal clergy whom most of us have contact with, though today most of us know deacons as well. We probably only get to see the bishop on special occasions such as confirmations, but hopefully these situations stir something up inside us, if for no other reason than we get to put a face to the name we hear each week at Sunday Mass. Holy Orders is the first "team ministry" in the history of the Church. The bishop oversees the work of the local church, called a diocese, and that diocese is divided into the parishes to which we all belong. The parishes are run by priests who are assisted in their work by deacons, religious brothers and sisters, and lay ministers.

We are a sacramental people, established precisely because we have all been baptized. It makes sense, therefore, that those called to lead us should be set apart by a special sacrament. This sacrament we call Holy Orders, because those who receive it are called to order and direct the work of the Church. It is a sacrament of service and leadership, not of privilege or pride. The deacon represents this aspect of service especially as he serves at the altar just as a waiter does at a table. Even his stole is worn over one shoulder, just as waiters in high end restaurants and wine stewards to this day wear a stole over their left shoulder. The priest signifies ministry and leadership from within the people. He is the one ordained to celebrate the Mass, to offer the holy sacrifice of Christ and to instruct the Christian faithful. Because it is important to celebrate the Eucharist worthily, and because we are wounded by sin, the priest is also empowered to forgive sins in the sacrament of penance. Sickness and death touch all of us too, hence the power to anoint. Bishops represent headship because they oversee not only the local parish, but the whole local church. For this reason bishops are the only ones empowered to pass on the power of Orders itself. This means they are the only ones who can ordain priests and deacons for service to that local church. Bishops are also typically the ones to confirm, though any priest can do it with permission. Bishops prefer to perform this sacrament themselves, however, because it ensures not only that they visit every parish occasionally, but that they get to meet everyone in their diocese at least once. You see, there's a practical living out of one's vocation even as a bishop!

Obviously deacons, priests, and bishops are human beings, and it can be tempting to think that all of this business about Holy Orders is just second-century management principles, but nothing could be further from the truth. The early Church certainly recognized the distinct roles of deacon, bishop, and priest, but it did so because it believed them to have been given by Christ himself. "See that you all follow the Bishop, as Christ does the Father, and the priests as you would the apostles; and reverence the deacons, as a command of God." That's from Saint Ignatius of Antioch, who was writing around 111 AD, just a few years after the death of the last apostle. Holy Orders is a sacrament, not just because we say so, but because from the beginning the Church has been convinced that Christ said so.

The priesthood echoes the priesthood of the Old Testament, especially as it offers a sacrifice. But instead of offering livestock and cereal, our priests offer the holy body and blood of the Lord. And they help us to make offerings too: of our time, talent, and treasure, but especially of our whole lives. Our priests have a priesthood rooted in the one priesthood of Christ, which is ultimately about self-offering and mediation, about going between man and God and back again. The bishops aren't just regional managers or important priests; they actually stand in the place of the apostles. And our deacons, like Saint Stephen, who is martyred at the beginning of the Acts of the Apostles, are a special sign and a kind of icon to us of Christ the servant. They remind us that leadership in the Church is different in the rest of the world. That's why our priests and bishops are all ordained deacons first, to remind them that their ministry and their leadership is one of service and not self-interest. Holy Orders helps to make the ordering, direction, and management of the Church holy.

The mistake that we often make about Holy Orders in general and about the priesthood in particular is thinking that the clergy are the professional religious people and therefore the work of evangelization is theirs alone. Again, nothing could be further from the truth. The clergy exist for the upbuilding and governance of the Church, but most of their work is done inside the Church. Most of the evangelization that needs to take place is not within the Church but outside its walls. This work falls precisely to everyday Christians, to ordinary old laypeople, both married and unmarried, to do the bulk of that work. Priests help to continually reconvert the Church and to receive those converts that the laity have already made, but the bulk of the work of making new Christians, of establishing a Christian culture and of changing the world, falls not to bishops, priests, and deacons, but to us. But let us not forget that our work would be impossible were it not for them, so we should encourage and support them in every way we can, pray for them, and pray for vocations to the priesthood and religious life to help support us in our work.

LIVING IN A SACRAMENTAL FAMILY

Like any family, somebody has to be in charge of this sacramental family. That's what the bishops, and on a more local level the priests, are for. As discussed earlier, it's why we call them Father. The spiritual fatherhood of the priesthood is one of the greatest gifts Christ has given to his Church, which the Church passes on to her people. Our priests do for us as a Church what we as parents do for our own kids: They teach us the faith, offer us good examples, help remind us what makes us part of this family. They feed us, literally, with the Eucharist and give of themselves absolutely. This is one of the major reasons that priests cannot be married. They are married to all of us in the Church. They are available twenty-four hours a day, seven days a week, 365 days a year. They stay up all night with sick parishioners just like we stay up all night with sick kids. They visit the nursing homes to look after the elderly members of the family just like we go to see Grandma and Grandpa at the nursing home. They help us to raise our kids and give us advice on everything from sex to work to school. They are, in short, everything a father is supposed to be.

Priests are heads of the family because they are first members of that family. Our spiritual fathers are first Christians themselves, which means they are first repentant sinners. We have a right to expect a good example from our priests just as we have a right to expect reasonable behavior from our dads, but our priests, like our dads, can reasonably expect us to be gentle and forgiving as they struggle with human weakness. Our priests aren't perfect and we can't expect them to be, but how we treat them can go a long way toward motivating them on the way to perfection.

If the priests are the "fathers," then who are the "mothers" in the Church? Well, strictly speaking, the Church is herself our mother. Baptismal fonts are made to resemble not only tombs but also wombs, and so the Church gives birth to new Christians with the sacraments she celebrates. Because the priests are the ones who gather the people and who are ordained by God to stand in the place of Christ for the community, they are called Father. Saint Paul did this himself. For this reason priests are said to be married to the Church—that is, all of us. Mother types come to us, naturally enough, then, from women in the Church. Women from a variety of vocations and life situations often wind up "mothering" the rest of us in the Church. We all know the woman of the parish, or a friend in general, who listens to us in our struggles and gives us the care and love that only a mother can. But in a very special way women religious play a mothering role for the whole Church as well.

Religious women, both cloistered nuns and active sisters, make promises of celibate chastity just like priests and male religious do. The symbolism of their promise is different, however, for while the priest is said to be married to the Church, the woman religious is married to Christ himself. Women religious especially, but also widowed women who aren't necessarily responsible for their own families anymore, have a special role to "mother" in the Church. They nurture, guide, support, and challenge us as only a mother can. And I can tell you from the years I spent in seminary and the many priest friends I have still that those who often appreciate this mothering most are the priests themselves.

A number of years ago Dan Brown came out with the conspiracy thrillers *The Da Vinci Code* and *Angels and Demons*. One of the gimmicks he used in the books to try and cast suspicion on Christianity as a whole and Catholicism in particular was to point out the sexual imagery "coded" in ancient churches. He wrote about phallic steeples and womb-shaped sanctuaries like they were something new, and he suggested that the erotic poses that artists sometimes use to show either martyrs in agony or mystics in ecstasy are some weird kind of sexual acting out on the part of celibate men. Of course, this is all just silly, not because sexual imagery isn't woven throughout the Church's art, architecture, and liturgy, but because it is there in plain view for all to see. Not only that, but it's an essential part of our teaching not only on the goodness of human sexuality, but more important on the closeness of Christ to his Church.

During the Easter vigil the deacon sings one of the Church's most ancient hymns, called the Exsultet, which is loaded with marital imagery for Christ and his Church. Then the priest blesses the new water for the baptismal font and the candle is plunged into the font again and again and again. Some of the most revered theologians in the Church have seen in this liturgical act of lovemaking a font that is now fertile, so that those who are baptized are not only ritually born again, but actually become new people by virtue of their baptism. This symbolism is not about the sexual frustrations of a celibate clergy. Rather, it's the very reason for having a celibate clergy; they become living signs, living sacraments to the rest of us of our true lives, which are not only lived in our homes and offices and ballparks and shopping centers, but in the Church and as members of the Church, and wherever else they may go.

FROM GENERATION TO GENERATION

The Church is called "catholic" not simply to differentiate itself from Episcopalians, Presbyterians, and Methodists, but because it is universal. That's what the word means in Greek. So there is one, holy, universal, and apostolic Church because the Church is meant to take in members from every race, age, nationality , and way of life.

Sure, you can have young parishes and old parishes, parishes with more funerals than baptisms or more Sunday Schoolers than people over fifty but generally speaking, most every parish, even a Newman Center or college campus ministry, will have people young and old. Where else in our regular lives would five-year-

96

olds be forced to interact in a meaningful way with eighty-five-year-olds? Besides your own grandparents, what other old people do you relate to when you're twelve? And especially with more and more people living far away from home and family, the old people at the parish can wind up serving as surrogate grandparents for the young and the young at heart.

Though society often brushes them aside, the elderly have a critical role to play in the life of the Church. The sacrament of anointing makes ritually clear what is already the case: that everyone who suffers does so within and through the suffering of Christ. The aches and pains of old age have been sanctified just as much as the bumps and scrapes of childhood by the miracle of the Incarnation. The great work that the elderly perform just by being old is of infinite value to the whole Church and the whole world. This is in stark contrast to what popular culture has to say about the elderly. In the Church we don't hide our elders away to focus on the young. Nor do we consider them of lesser value because they can't work anymore. In the Providence of God the prayers, penance, and pain of the old very likely make possible the grace-filled lives of the young.

Not only that, but the biblical witness is clear that old age is a sign, not so much of God's favor, but rather of the wisdom of experience. We should rely confidently on the experience of the elderly. We should heed their advice and the wisdom that life has given them, listening and learning from the stories they share. One of the great gifts the Church gives the elderly is to take them seriously. Encouraging frequent confession and communion on the part of the elderly indicates our common recognition that nobody ever stops growing, and that the journey to Christian perfection lasts a lifetime, however long that may be.

PATIENCE, PERSEVERANCE, AND PERFECTION

One of the arguments you hear a lot against Christianity in general, and Catholicism in particular, is that we're all a bunch of hypocrites. We get together on Sunday mornings, some of us in really fancy robes, and we pretend to be holy, while the rest of the week we act just like everybody else. There are two problems with this. The first is that if we are always acting just like everybody else, then we aren't being very consistent with our Catholic witness. But the second problem is probably even more important, and that's simply that our critics have misunderstood us. We don't get together on Sunday mornings to act holy—we get together so that someday, after a long life of prayer and Christian fellowship and good works and all the rest, we might actually be holy. That's what the sacraments are meant to help us accomplish, that's what the communion of the Church is actually for, and that's the whole point of actually being a Christian in the first place. If we're pretending to be holy, then it's surely because we already aren't. The point is to be trying.

Everybody knows that scandals have rocked the Church, and especially the priesthood, for at least the past ten years or so. The truth is that the Church has had scandals from the very beginning. In fact, the whole mystery of the salvation is tied up with the scandal of Judas's betrayal of Jesus—and remember, Judas was an apostle, the first generation of bishops; we shouldn't be surprised that some of our people go bad now too. Whenever a scandal hits the Church it affects everyone, and rightfully so. That is why the Church's call to conversion is all the more important. We in our families must pray for that same conversion each day and live by it the best we can.

We need to cultivate an attitude of patience toward ourselves and our families first, and then to the rest of the Church, so that we can actually grow in the Christian life and not just feel lousy all the time. We need to learn to offer correction and to be corrected, but to do both with such love that both parties can't help but be better for it. This is as true if you are five as it is if you are 105, and it's the reason for every single one of us crossing the threshold of our parish each week. It's what makes us Catholic. And in the end, it's what's going to save us.

A MOST CHRISTIAN VIRTUE

OBEDIENCE TRAINING

If you've ever seen one of my talks, then you know that *quiet* and *reserved* are not words that people usually use to describe me. I'm a pretty straightforward guy, both at the microphone and away from it. Sometimes my wife wishes I'd be less so, especially when having new guests over for dinner. Truth be told, though, she loves it. In fact, it was an important part of how she fell in love with me.

You see, I gave her a short book on our first date. A small gift might not be quite so gutsy, but it was on the topic of the theology of the body, John Paul II's revolutionary teaching on the sacredness of human sexuality and the natural complementarity of the sexes. Then I told her something like, "This book says everything that I want to say about how I want this relationship to work. So read it, and if you don't like it, don't bother to call me back, and you can keep the book." Okay, I realize that may have been coming on a little strong for a first date, but apparently it worked.

It took her only a few days to read the book, and on our third date Teresa brought it up herself. "It totally blew my mind!" She said that she'd never read anything quite like it. And what was more, "It just made sense to me." It offered her not only an answer, but a whole-scale alternative to the freewheeling sexual culture in which we all live. And she decided that this was what she wanted out of a relationship too. It's no surprise that we wound up getting married.

Teresa's heart was moved by what she read, just as mine had been earlier (though probably more from what I'd heard), and so we were delighted to obey. This is, in the best of circumstances, how obedience is supposed to work. We hear (or read) what God may be asking us to do, we ponder it, bounce it off of those we trust, and then, because we love God, we take delight in doing it. Of course, for most of us obedience is usually a little bit tougher sell than all that, but it's important to know the ideal.

LISTEN UP!

My Latin isn't very good (and I even took four years in high school), but I have some close friends who can talk like Cicero or Saint Augustine. They tell me that the English word obedience comes from the Latin *ob + audire*. Now, even I can see that this means it's related to hearing somehow. I guess it means "to listen" or "to listen really hard." But to what are we called to listen? To whom? And how are we to respond in obedient faith?

Even secular psychologists tell us that listening is different from simply hearing. I can hear someone talking but am not necessarily able to tell you what he's said. Listening requires something more. It's a holy kind of listening, a devout sort of practice that is open to being changed by what is said.

This change is only possible if we're willing to hear what's being said in context. Who is speaking? What's my relationship to him? How is he speaking? Why is he saying this? And what does this have to do with the rest of the faith as a whole?

That's all kind of abstract. Let's give a concrete example. When I set up speaking engagements, I first run by Teresa all of the other obligations we have for the coming year: family vacations, visits to relatives, weddings, graduations, and any other potential conflicts. Between our social lives and my work schedule we have very, very few weekends free. Occasionally one of these free weekends will approach, a weekend that we haven't planned out, and one of my buddies will say, "Hey, how 'bout we head to the lake to go boating for the weekend? It would be like a guys' trip away for a few days!" Now, my inclination is, of course, to go. I know that I should check with Teresa first, but I'm afraid that if I do she'll say no and then I'll be stuck, so I agree. But later on when I'm home and I tell her that after all I will be away for the weekend, she's upset. She asks me not to go. The better form of obedience would be simply to have not agreed to go in the first place. A lesser but still good form of obedience would be to at that point cancel on my buddies, even if it means that they are going to be disappointed and angry. To persist in going, though, would be disobedient, and it would be disobedient to the most important person in my life—my wife.

Obedience is about a very intentional sort of listening, but it always happens within the context of a relationship. We owe obedience to some people and not to others, and we owe a different kind of obedience to different people in our lives. Religious, of course, take a formal vow of obedience, and diocesan priests promise obedience to their bishop. But married people have a kind of primary obedience to each other, which is why Saint Paul is always telling people to be mutually subordinate to one another.

We promise love and fidelity to our spouses at our weddings.

Most of us manage to do so without a whole lot of effort, at least a lot of the time. But that's because fidelity to marriage vows often consists of simply not cheating on your spouse. Of course, we all know that to have a successful marriage, even just to stay married, will require a lot more than sexual or emotional fidelity. It is very much like the priest or religious: The vows provide a kind of outer boundary for the life, but what makes it all work is something much, much deeper than simply not breaking the rules.

For those of us who are married, our vows come into play every time we engage our relationship with our spouses. Doing our share of the housework, coming home on time after work, maintaining good boundaries with friends and family, and being attentive to the emotional needs of our spouses are all acts of obedience. So are those acts of kindness that simply help to reinforce the marriage bond. For instance, Teresa likes for me to keep my office clean. She's rarely in my office, almost never works there, and in one way needn't have any say over how I keep it, but I do my best to keep it clean and orderly because I know that she likes it that way. It's a simple act that helps me to be more obedient and is a sure way of expressing my love.

The best models of obedience most of us know are our own children. As kids we nearly have to be obedient, because the grown-ups all know so much more than we do. Whether we are married or unmarried, priest or religious, the vows we take help define the outer limits of our lives, help us to know when we've strayed too far. But within those bounds the limits are endless, and the practice of staying within those boundaries helps us to develop the virtue of obedience itself.

THE VIRTUE OF CHRIST

In the Letter to the Philippians, Saint Paul records what most scholars believe is perhaps the most ancient Christian hymn. It's a common second reading at Sunday Mass and is sung by priests and religious every Saturday night. It should sound familiar:

Though he was in the form of God, did not regard equality with God something to be grasped. Rather, he emptied himself, taking the form of a slave, coming in human likeness; and found human in appearance, he humbled himself, becoming obedient to death, even death on a cross. Because of this, God greatly exalted him and bestowed on him the name that is above every name, that at the name of Jesus every knee should bend, of those in heaven and on earth and under the earth, and every tongue confess that Jesus Christ is Lord, to the glory of God the Father. (Phil. 2:6–11)

Cultivating the virtue of obedience, even as Christ had it, is the real goal of vows, whether in marriage or in religious life. The goal is to be humble and obedient, and so to conform yourself better to the will of God. This is some of the hardest work of the Christian life, but it will make us most Christlike.

This also fits in better with Christ's own vision of obedience, which is never blind submission to the law but observance of the law with the end in mind. Just think of how many times he healed on the Sabbath or didn't wash his hands. He never omitted a practice when it was important, but he got on the Pharisees harder than anybody else because they clung so closely to the letter of the law that they wound up being disobedient to its intention.

The purpose of the law is to cultivate virtue, and the purpose of virtue is to instill in us good character and a right intention.

Sometimes we think that if we're good we go to heaven when we die because we've got a clean record. It's really much more like we choose heaven at the point of our death because we've become the sort of people who would want to spend eternity with God. Obedience is the basis of this relationship, which sees God for who he is in our lives and sees us as we really are, right now, and not simply as we might like to be.

This is why the *Catechism of the Catholic Church* relates obedience to faith:

143. *By faith,* man completely submits his intellect and his will to God. With his whole being man gives his assent to God the revealer. Sacred Scripture calls this human response to God, the author of revelation, "the obedience of faith."

144. To obey (from the Latin *ob-audire,* to "hear or listen to") in faith is to submit freely to the word that has been heard, because its truth is guaranteed by God, who is Truth itself. Abraham is the model of such obedience offered us by Sacred Scripture. The Virgin Mary is its most perfect embodiment.

Obedience is ultimately rooted in faith. This is because it is based upon a relationship. All obedience begins with a relationship of trust between the superior and the subject. This is why all obedience is ultimately to God and not to the human superior who represents him. It is also why we are able to respond in faith to the call to obedience to some action that we do not understand. And it's why it is so important that people with others subject to them, either in the Church or outside of it, work to cultivate the trust of those in their charge.

WHO'S ON FIRST?

One of the hardest things about obedience is that we are all called to be obedient to different people, but sometimes they tell us wildly different things. Sometimes this is pretty benign, like when we're kids and Mom says we can't do something but Dad lets us do it. Other times, though, it can be really confusing and cause genuine moral turmoil. What do I do if my pastor asks me to do one thing but I know that the pope has said another? What if the government demands something of me that I believe to be immoral? What if my wife asks for something particular in a situation but my confessor suggests something different? Just whom am I bound to obey?

First, there's the Church. Jesus passed on his authority to his apostles, and to Peter in particular. "I say to you, you are *Peter*, and upon this rock I will build my Church, and the gates of the netherworld shall not prevail against it." The pope is the direct successor to Saint Peter himself, and the bishops of the Catholic Church stand in the place of the apostles. Jesus continues his ministry in the Church today through the bishops of the Church, especially under the leadership of the Holy Father. We're bound to what they say because we're bound to Christ. Just as we don't always understand why he asks what he does of us, we don't always understand what the Church demands of us, but because we love Christ and because we love the Church, we obey.

But Church authority isn't the only kind with its roots in the authority of God. As early as Saint Paul, the Church recognized that the civil government, so long as it was acting in recognizably legitimate ways, had real authority that Christians were bound to obey. From the earliest days of the Church prayers for the emperor, then the prevailing civil authority, as well as the senate, were included in the Church's liturgy. This wasn't about some sort of pagan influence in the Church. Far from it, pagan Romans wouldn't pray for the emperor because they revered him as a god. But Christians prayed *for* the emperor and the empire, despite being constantly persecuted and frequently killed for the faith.

Civil authority today still holds such authority. So long as a government is legitimate and recognized as such by both its citizens and by the governments of other nations, then in principle the authority of the government is to be respected and obeyed. In the United States this means that we need to have a healthy respect for the office of the presidency, for our Congress and Senate, and our judiciary. It means that we should engage the political process and use our votes to the best of our ability to make sure that the best people are elected to these most important positions. It also means that we have to make our voices heard, even as the early Christians did, in the face of oppression or unjust laws. Sometimes this may mean actually breaking or at least refusing to comply with some edict of the government. This can entail consequences for us just as it did for the early Christians. Like them, however, we cannot enter into such a situation lightly. We must first be as reasonably sure of our position as we can be, and then pray over the best and most prudent way not to follow the wicked law.

Church history abounds with examples of Christians who faced imprisonment, torture, and even death rather than follow and unjust civil law. Probably the best known is the saint Sir Thomas More. He's important for us today because he was a Catholic politician, and it was his commitment to the Catholic faith as a politician that cost him his freedom and ultimately his life. More refused to sign the oath of supremacy that would recognize the king as the head of the Church in England. He easily could have. No one during that time would have blamed him. All but one of the bishops in the country did. So did most of the priests. And all of Parliament. And every member of his family. But More stuck to his guns. He refused to sign the oath. Even as he went to his death Thomas More recognized the legitimate authority of the king, while at the same time maintaining that the law was wicked. For this reason he told the crowd gathered for his execution that he was "the king's good servant, but God's first." That's what we have to be: good, righteous, and holy citizens, but faithful Christians first.

Of course, there are other people in each of our lives to whom we also owe obedience. We never really stop being our parents' children, and the command to honor them doesn't disappear once we turn eighteen or twenty-one or even sixty-one. At the same time, our obedience to our parents certainly shifts as time goes on, and especially as we embark upon our own vocations. For most of us, the person to whom we owe our primary obedience is our husband or wife. We have to be mutually subject to one another, as Saint Paul has said, so that together we can grow in holiness as well as be open to the grace that God longs to give us through the will of our spouse. But we also have an obligation to be obedient to our supervisors at work, insofar as work stuff goes, and our doctors as regards our health, and other people like this in our lives.

Just as we (hopefully) obey our doctors in regard to our physical health, and Mom and Dad in regard to societal behavior, we obey the Church in regard to our spiritual well-being. Though I may not necessarily like eating light dressing, having one portion of rigatoni, and exercising, I know that this is ultimately what is best for the good of my body, according to my doctor. To be honest, I'd like to scream every once in a while as I wait for the slowest cashier in the world to get to my groceries, but my parents taught me when I was young that it wouldn't get me very far. So too with our souls. Though following our Church's teachings and our pastor's moral direction can at times be difficult, we should remain confident that this is where our true freedom and purpose rest. Further, this way of living, in which we give our lives to Jesus Christ as Catholics, is exactly the example of love we should be showing our kids and our spouses.

I am reminded each time I enter a church of what the life of a Christian is all about. How could I miss it? It's hanging right in front of me. The crucifix is where I find the truest example of love, in Christ giving his life for me, my kid, my parents, and my wife, and darn it, I'm going to make it my mission for me and my family to try and give everything we can back.

THE EXTENDED FAMILY

A BAG OF MIXED NUTS

The Church is a dynamic reality, composed of old and young, weak and strong, rich and poor, sinners and saints. This last, however, is the most important, and the lesson every member can teach to every other. The Church is full of both sinners and saints, but the thing to remember about saints is that they are all first redeemed sinners. The sacraments we celebrate and the faith we share are what help make us better and what draw us closer to God and to one another.

So just as with our own families, the Church is a pretty mixed bag. Some people have hard shells and others wear their feelings on their sleeves. Some people are totally dedicated and others are always half-skeptical. Some people are obviously holy and others are obviously faking, but most of us are somewhere in between. The point is that the Church in our homes, especially the local parish, offers all of us the opportunity to meet with and engage a whole series of people we would never see otherwise and so to grow from the experience. In the end, that's what the mysteries of faith we celebrate are for—to show us who we really are, and so bring us closer to God, our families, and to each other.

MORE THAN MEETS THE EYE

Every family is bigger than it first appears to be. Of course you've got Mom and Dad and the kids living at home, and these people are certainly your primary or nuclear family, but the people who make up your family include much more than these alone. You've got grandparents and aunts and uncles and cousins of every sort. In an earlier generation it was more common for some of these people to live together; your primary family might have included your folks and siblings, your grandparents, and maybe another set of aunts, uncles, and cousins. Some ethnic groups and recent immigrants still do this, and it's not uncommon at all for people to have a grandparent or two living with them, at least when they get older. Don't underestimate the impact that your extended family can have on the way you live your daily life, and especially on how you think of yourself and your family.

We all have very special family members as well. Whether these were part of our nuclear family or of a more extended variety, those bound to us by blood who have died are also part of our families, and their impact, good or bad, far outlasts their lives lived on earth. In some mysterious way they continue to be part of our families, even part of our daily lives, and so are part of our faith too. We can't forget them.

The same is true of the family of the Church. We have the local parish, which is something like our primary family. The pastor serves as the "father" of the parish and any additional priests, deacons, and pastoral staff all share the paternal role. At the same time most of the parishioners are going to be adults, which simply means that Father needs to make sure that he has grown-up children. Then we have the bishop, whom we probably don't see often but for whom we should have special affection. He's something very much like the grandfather of the diocese. The pope, then, is like the patriarch of all of these families. That means the people in the neighboring parish are something like your cousins in the faith. This should be part of the reason, at least, that you feel comfortable in a Catholic church whether it's across town or across the globe.

Most famously, though, in the family of the Church we have many, many members who have preceded us in faith—our spiritual ancestors, if you will. These are the saints, and what makes up the relationship between your parish and the other parishes in the city, as well as between you and all of the righteous dead, is what we call the communion of saints. That's not just a fancy phrase we use in the creed; it's the glue that holds God's family together. This great communion of Christians living and dead is the mark of the Church's unity. We depend upon one another for prayers, rely upon one another for support, and look to one another and together with them to Christ to find the source of our identity as Christians, as spouses, and as parents.

CLOSE, CLOSER, CLOSEST

We're called to love each other, right? We're called to love good and bad people. Love he poorest of the poor and the most unrepentant criminal. Love those who can't speak for themselves to those who can. My favorite phrase for this is "from womb to tomb." But does that mean we have to love all people equally? I mean, you say, "I love you," to your spouse each night before bed (if you don't then you should start right now), but does that mean the same thing as when you say, "I love the people we feed at the homeless shelter," or when the parish declares that it "loves" the latest victims of some horrible natural disaster? Well, yes and no.

We are called to love all people as best as we can, but that doesn't mean that we need to relate to all people in just the same way. Jesus forgave everyone who had a part in his death—he even said so; it was only to Peter that he offered a formal reconciliation after the Resurrection.

Saint Thomas Aquinas, who was one of the smartest guys who ever lived and one of the most stellar Catholics in history, talked about the "hierarchy of love." While we certainly love everyone the same in that we wish good for them and eternal happiness in the end, both the intensity of our affection and the compelling power of our actions are ordered according to a kind of natural preference. We are bound to love first our spouses and those related to us by blood , then extended family, then our friends, our fellow citizens, and the citizens of other nations. The point is that while the bonds of faith, hope, and love really do unite us with everybody, they don't unite us with everyone equally. In fact, part of what binds me in love to the starving child in Sudan is precisely my love for my wife and mother.

This has some pretty serious implications, especially when it comes to raising our kids. We have to first teach them what it means to be loved by loving them, along with our spouses, as much as and as best we can. Then we can teach them how to love by showing them what acts of charity look like among family members, friends, and neighbors. Finally we can teach them how to love globally and universally by showing them the importance of giving to charity and by modeling service to our parish. Our most serious obligation is to teach our kids the faith, and this means not just teaching them the doctrinal content but also showing them what it looks like in action.

All of the Church's teachings have consequences, even if they're not immediately obvious. The dogma of Mary's Assumption, that she was received body and soul into heaven, seems like a quirky piece of trivia. It's not. It tells us just how much God loves and respects our bodies, and it demands that we treat our own bodies and those of others with equal respect. From the teaching on the Assumption, which is just a logical consequence of the Resurrection of Jesus, we get everything from the practice of burying the dead to the veneration of relics.

Every single one of our teachings can come alive in this way, but only if we take the opportunity to engage with the teachings. Do you chat with your kids about Father's homily in the car on the way home? Do you remember what the intentions were at Mass last Sunday? Do you pray them at home? We all play little games with our kids to help them memorize things, but do we ever organize games to help them learn the faith? And how do we model really important things like forgiveness and reconciliation? If we have a fight with our spouse in front of the kids, do we make sure to apologize and ask forgiveness, also in front of the kids? When we help our little ones to make up after a spat with a sibling or friend, do we make sure they know that we do so not just because Mom or Dad says so, but because Jesus taught us to? And do we pass on the stories, wit, and wisdom of those special members of God's family whom we call the saints? Do we show by our words and example the special love we have for God's holy ones, the desire that we have to be like them, and so stir up the same in our kids?

SPECIAL CASES

Of course, every family has those "special cases": members who get special consideration because of age, illness, or sometimes just plain orneriness. Well, in the family of the Church we have those special cases too. You see, as we come to love God more we learn not only to love our neighbors better but also to love those whom God loves especially—namely, the saints. The saints are those special friends of God whom we are called to love in a very particular way, what the Church calls "devotion." Devotion to the saints is a bit like special affection for great uncles or aunts. It's not that you love them more than your own close kin, exactly, but more that by loving them especially you come to see what makes them special and so can better emulate them on your way to God.

There are different ways of doing this. Obviously a good place to start is to learn about the patron saint of your parish. So if you belong to a parish called St. Theresa's, try learning something about her life. Read a biography or visit with someone who might know something about her. If your parish is named not after a saint but rather after some great mystery of the faith, like Holy Trinity or Sacred Heart, ask the pastor how the place got its name. There are typically saints associated with all of these devotions. Getting to know your namesake or the saint whose name you took at confirmation is a good beginning point as well.

Sometimes the best saints to get to know are the ones who aren't official yet.]This can be as simple as asking for stories at a family reunion of your pious great-grandmother Sophia. Other times it means getting stories and learning about famous Catholics from your area. Oftentimes local causes or movements have already begun the process of getting the person made a saint, but if there isn't one it just might be your prompting that gets it started. I know where I'm from the first priest in the state is about to be declared "Blessed," which is just one step away from being made a saint. And the founding pastor of a parish nearby lived in the sacristy the first ten years so that he could build a school. These special people positively surround us.

AN OPEN DOOR

Some families are very private. Family gatherings are reserved for those related by blood only, and sometimes even in-laws are a questionable addition. Other families are very open. I remember this family that lived right across the street from our parish school when I was a kid. Their door was always open. Other kids were constantly coming and going and the mom just had a way of making you feel at home, like this was your safe place too. There are positives and negatives to both approaches, but the Church is definitely more like the second family described than like the first one.

You see, the Church as a family is constantly growing. Our members are related by blood—not their own blood, but the blood of Jesus. This means that every member is to be constantly on the lookout for other people interested in becoming part of our family. There's a real intimacy that develops here, especially since so much of what we do as a family at church is pray together. But it also instills in us a kind of attitude toward the outside world. We shouldn't be constantly on guard, though there are obviously things we need to protect ourselves from. Instead, we should be forever inviting the world in, so that those who currently live outside the Church can see better what they're missing, and those who do belong to the Church, but only halfheartedly, can see how much better their lives can still be.

The Church's history is full of the stories of various people we've invited in. One of the most famous is the great Saint Augustine. His mother, Saint Monica, was a Catholic but his father was a pagan. Monica spent years praying for her son's conversion and nagging him every chance she got. He did what every self-respecting young man would do: He ignored her with impunity.

He went off to a college town, got very drunk, moved in with a girl, and for a while even joined a cult. But eventually, after years and years of invitation and being dragged to Mass occasionally, it all clicked. Then the sermons of the one priest friend he'd made, a man called Ambrose, began to make sense. Then his mother's devotion began to fit. Then his life was changed absolutely, irrevocably, forever. And the thing is, the Church and the world were changed by it too. Augustine became a bishop and the greatest theologian of his age. He helped see the Church through a very difficult period and clarified a number of errors that had become full-blown heresies. Perhaps most important of all, he left us a little book known as Confessions. This is a kind of spiritual autobiography in which he is very clear about his own sin and sinfulness but uses even that to tell the story of his conversion and to give greater glory to God. Saint Augustine remains one of the greatest examples of what can happen when we actually take the gospel seriously.

ALMOST HEROES

We all need heroes. Every summer Hollywood wows us with blockbuster movies featuring people who can fly, caped crusaders kicking the butts of criminals, and unlikely enlisted people who turn out to be not only super soldiers but also astounding orators and world-class lovers. And we follow their antics, not because we believe that they're real or true or factual, but because we recognize in their spirit something that is deep and true and beautiful. We don't believe in the adventures so much as we believe in the heroes themselves, and in believing in them we hope somehow to become like them ourselves.

In a more natural way we develop our own heroes in political and social life. War heroes almost always have an easier time getting elected than ordinary citizens. Star athletes are natural role models for our kids, especially if in addition to their physical skills they've had to overcome serious personal hardships, and who isn't moved by the stories of plain folk who gave their lives to save a stranger's, whether on September 11th, in the movie theater in Colorado, or just during a regular old mugging in Chicago? Heroes remind us of what we can all be, while inspiring us to grow.

In the Church we have heroes too; they're called "saints." The saints aren't just people who live in stained-glass windows or wear fancy old clothes. These are really just the trading-card images. No, the saints are those heroes in the faith whose lives we admire and whose example we imitate because they stir up the best in us. We admire what they can do and wish that we could do it ourselves, and they help us to believe that we can. That's why any healthy spiritual life is going to include a devotion to the saints in general and to some special saints in particular. It's also why every parent should be sure to introduce their children to a whole variety of saints just as they would expose them to a variety of sports figures, superheroes, and other role models. Providing your kids with healthy heroes is one of the most important tasks in helping them to grow up.

THE SAINTS:
YESTERDAY, TODAY, AND FOREVER

Many Catholics today practically ignore the saints, and I mean what I say: practically, in practice. They find the saints to be simply dead people from a long-distant time who have little to no relevance to today. They're good, if we're lucky, for special foods on feast days and helping us to pick out baby names—maybe. But these people are missing out on so much. The saints are vital and alive, and we surely have saints running around today. The question is: Do we know how to spot them? And better, what should we do with them when we find them?

The word *saint* comes from the Latin word *sanctus* which means "holy." A saint, then, is simply a holy person. The apostle Paul uses the word saints more than seventy times in the New Testament. He refers to all Christians as saints, not because they are all especially holy, but because as Christians they are members of a "holy people." The Church certainly still teaches that we are all holy in the sense of belonging to God's holy people, but very early on it developed the language of the communion of saints as found in the ancient creeds. This was meant primarily to refer to those departed members of the Church who now live with Christ in glory.

These days we tend to reserve the word *saints* for the dead, and in particular for those dead Christians whose lives and deaths have left an especially compelling example for the rest of us. We talk about these men and women as models of "heroic virtue." It doesn't mean that they were perfect or never sinned themselves—far from it—but rather that their own growth in holiness and virtue and the way in which they overcame sin and vice in their own lives is a worthy example for the rest of us to follow.

In the early days saints were typically determined by popular piety. This means that the people themselves simply recognized who was holy and began to venerate them on their own following their deaths. This was especially true of martyrs in the early Church. Martyrdom, or dying for the faith, was seen as such a profound act of witness to Christ that the way a person actually lived was a secondary concern. Even after the great persecutions ended and most Christians died warm in their beds, it was the people who primarily "named" their own saints. As such, most of the earliest saints of the Church have never been formally named. It was only as time went on that an official Church process, now known as canonization, developed. This is basically designed to make sure that Christians don't accidentally start holding up as an example someone who is really unworthy of our veneration. The process is somewhat complicated, but it basically involves a thorough investigation into the lives of individuals to determine whether or not they did live lives of truly heroic virtue. If they are found to be so then they are typically declared "servant of God" (after this they are called "venerable"). Following this, miracles are sought out by their intercession. After the first miracle they are beatified (and so called "blessed") and prayers are written up for the celebration of their feast day at Mass, to be celebrated at least locally. Finally these people are canonized (and so declared saints) and their feast becomes available for a wider celebration in the Church.

There's nothing magic about this process. It's just a very commonsense way to distinguish those Christians worthy of the attention of the rest of the Church. The deeper and far more important truth is that the communion of saints is made up of three groups: the church militant, the church suffering, and the church triumphant. We, the living, make up the church militant, because we are still fighting, still striving for the prize. The church suffering are the souls of those faithful Christians already in Purgatory awaiting only their final purification before being admitted to heaven. And the church triumphant are the saints, those already in heaven with God enjoying eternal friendship with Christ. That is, of course, the end goal for all of us and the most important thing we can strive for.

LIKE A MAN FROM OLDEN TIMES

Like a lot of Catholics, for a long time I didn't have any real devotion to any particular saints. I mean, I'd gone to St. Pius X grade school and I knew that he was a pope who had something to do with first Communion, and I'd certainly done reports on saints sometimes for class, like when I got confirmed. But I never had anyone I turned to regularly, except maybe Saint Anthony when I'd lose my wallet. But when I got to high school all of that changed.

I was on a bus ride coming back from a band trip. There was an older student on the bus who was kind of a pious guy and who took a lot of flack about it from the other kids. But this guy was also a terrific storyteller, and that night he was telling stories about the saints. He'd just come back from a Mass in which they'd blessed the people with Padre Pio's glove. He talked all about Padre Pio and how the stories of his life made him sound like a man from olden times, but that he'd only died in 1968. In fact, this kid's dad had actually gone to see the good padre during a trip to Italy in college. At that time they were still working to get Padre Pio made a saint (he was, eventually, in 2002).

The way this kid talked really made this saint come alive for me. In some ways, he was a lot like the priests I knew back home. He was a poor farm kid from rural Italy, and most of the priests I knew in Iowa had come from relatively poor farm families. He'd had a sense of priesthood at an early age, and the first chance he got he went away to seminary. It turned out Padre Pio was a Franciscan. But what was really amazing about the story this kid was telling was that even though Padre Pio was a lot like the people I knew, and even though he'd died within living memory, his life read like that of some medieval saint. He frequently fell into spiritual ecstasy in his prayers and couldn't be drawn out of it, even by physical pain. He heard confessions for hours a day, and hundreds of people report the phenomenon known as "soul reading." This means that Padre Pio was able to "see" and tell them their sins even if they hadn't confessed them. There are numerous reports of bilocation, which means being in two places at the same time. Dozens of healings were attributed to his prayers and blessings, even during his lifetime. Most famously, Padre Pio was known to have the visible wounds of the stigmata—the wounds of Christ in his hands and feet and side—for more than fifty years.

The stigmata may have made Padre Pio famous, but it also caused him a great deal of trouble. He was met with a ton of skepticism both within the Church and outside of it, and he had to undergo humiliating and painful medical examinations and observation for most of his life. For a time he was forbidden to hear confessions and say Mass publicly, and for most of his life he had to wear special fingerless gloves that would cover his wounds but allow him to perform his priestly functions. But in the midst of all this he was a renowned confessor. People would come from all over the world to seek his advice in the confessional. And he was something of a matchmaker, having helped to set up any number of good Catholic couples. He was also a great supporter of priestly and religious vocations, and reportedly said fairly prophetic things to the very young John Paul II.

What really amazed me about all of this, though, was that it really had just happened. I mean, both of my parents were alive in 1968. All the stories that we'd heard about the saints as kids— people levitating in prayer, reading other people's minds, casting out demons, fasting for years, and even the stigmata itself—these were still happening. So then the advice that Padre Pio gave out suddenly seemed really important, and had the authority of a saint. He recommended weekly confession, much like vacuuming out your room each week, and frequent communion to be nourished and fed. He often used to tell people, "Pray, hope, and don't worry." This was a kind of motto for him, and it became a kind of motto for me. Here was a very pastoral man, a modern man and a good priest, but one who was essentially a witness to the way the Church had always been.

Even though he could be hard on people, Padre Pio definitely had a sense of humor. The story goes that there was once a man who came to the village where Padre Pio was, to visit his sister who lived there. She convinced him to go to confession to the holy priest. By the time it was his turn he was pretty nervous and so made a very general and quick confession. Padre Pio, with both his supernatural ability to read souls and his experience reading people as a priest and confessor, said, "Isn't there something else?" The man flitzed and flutzed but essentially said no. Despite this, Padre Pio was keenly aware that the man's truck had broken down the day before on the way to the village and that he had sworn terribly. Now, in Italian most swear words are also blasphemous, and the worst sort have to do with the Blessed Virgin. Padre Pio chided him, "You've cursed your own mother! What did she ever do to your truck?" The man was moved and admitted the whole thing. He never swore blasphemous oaths after that.

Another story about Padre Pio that always moves me describes an event that occurred shortly after his death. There was an American sister teaching in a high school who was injured on the job. She was decorating for a school dance and fell off a ladder. Despite having no visible wounds, a short time later she developed a blood clot in her leg. Even with multiple surgeries the clots wouldn't go away, so the decision was made to amputate. The night before the surgery the superior of the convent discovered a box of holy cards to Padre Pio on the doorstep. He'd died only a few months before. The sisters kept vigil all night in prayer with the holy cards. The next morning when the doctors went in to do the surgery not only was the clot gone, but all evidence of the earlier surgeries had disappeared. This sister devoted much of the rest of her life to spreading devotion to Padre Pio. Years and years later she suffered a serious eye injury from a spring that popped out of a cushion. Again, she prayed for the intercession of Padre Pio, and not only was her sight restored, but it was better than ever before. Even in his healing Padre Pio had a sense of humor!

More than just stirring up a devotion to Padre Pio for me, however, this early experience of hearing stories about him turned me on to the saints in general. I began to read biographies of various saints, and whenever a feast would come by that would pique my interest, I'd try to find a book on the person. I explored Italian saints, of which there are many from the Middle Ages, to connect with my Italian heritage. I read about missionary saints and preacher saints, because I was drawn to preaching and evangelization. I loved the stories that told of miracles and other supernatural events in the lives of the saints. Most of all, though, I was drawn to those saints closest to our own time. I can remember when Mother Teresa and John Paul II were still alive, widely held to be living saints at the time. Little did I know just how close some living saints could be.

DELIGHTFULLY MODERN WOMAN

Another saint who has become really important for me, especially as my wife and I approach the birth of our first child, is Gianna Beretta Molla. She is a remarkable figure for a whole variety of reasons, not the least of which is that she was a wife and mother as well as a practicing physician. Her life of devoted service, and especially her death in light of serious opposition, is a beautiful testimony to the power of life and a mother's love, even in the face of death.

Gianna Francesca Beretta was born in Magenta, Italy, in 1922 (around the same time as my own grandparents). She was one of thirteen kids and so learned the value of children and family life very early on. As a girl she would tend injured animals and the neighbor kids as they got sick. She was also highly involved in her parish, the local youth group, and the St. Vincent de Paul Society. She went to college and then to medical school—pretty rare for a woman in the 1940s—and when she was finished set up a practice near Magenta. Much of her practice was occupied with the care of sick and needy children and their mothers. Gianna met a man who changed her life: Pietro Molla. They were a holy, happy couple and shared a common enthusiasm for life and service.

They were married in 1955 and blessed with children soon after. The busy work of a wife and mother and doctor soon came to occupy Gianna's life. Within four years they had three children and a fourth on the way. Life had changed dramatically for them, but they were living out their common vocation to marriage with dedication, enthusiasm, and a positively infectious joy.

In the course of her fourth pregnancy, however, something changed. Early on doctors discovered a fibroma in her uterus.

Given the state of medicine at the time, she had three options: abort her baby, have a hysterectomy, or have the fibroma removed, knowing that it could endanger her life. While abortion was obviously not an option, it's important to know that the hysterectomy could have been. Catholic moral teaching allows for a hysterectomy, even during pregnancy if the situation is serious enough. Operations, treatments, and medications that have as their direct purpose the cure of a proportionately serious pathological condition of a pregnant woman are permitted when they cannot be safely postponed until the unborn child is viable, even if they will result in the death of the unborn child." *(Ethical and Religious Directives for Catholic Health Care Services (ERD) Directive 45).* But Gianna, a doctor and mother and therefore more aware of the risks than anyone, said, "If you must choose between me and the baby, no hesitation; choose—and I demand it—the baby. Save her!"

She said this again and again and finally had a chance to put it into action. She chose to have the fibroma removed, and while the surgery was moderately successful, there were complications. By the time she had come to full term in her pregnancy, it was pretty clear that it was a matter of either Gianna or her child that would not survive. , Gianna insisted on her wishes that the baby shall live instead of her as she said, "the doctor should not meddle. The right of the child is equal to the right of the mother's life." And so, on Good Friday of 1962, she went into the hospital, where her youngest daughter, also called Gianna, was born via cesarean section. Despite the work of doctors, Gianna herself died of septic peritonitis just a week later. She kept whispering, "Jesus, I love you," right up to the end.

Gianna was canonized a saint in 2004 and has appropriately been made a special patron of the pro-life movement. Her husband and one of her daughters were actually able to be present at her canonization, the first time in history a husband has lived to see his wife canonized. I feel drawn to her, not only because of the way she died but also because of the way she lived. Women like Gianna are helpful for me because so many canonized saints are priests and religious. Gianna and her husband are both symbols of what real holiness can look like in married life.

In the ordinary day-to-day life of Saint Gianna is our family mission. I enjoy looking at pictures of her with Pietro and their family. Things like picnics in the park and family vacations suddenly come alive as occasions for grace and chances for the whole family to grow in holiness. The dedication she and her husband had, especially to the poor, the widowed, and the orphaned, is something that really moves me. It's like, "See, those meals you serve at the soup kitchen and the donations you bring to St. Vincent de Paul really do matter!" Like all good saints, she reminds me of what I'm capable of, of what Teresa and I can become because of our life together. I read every life of Saint Gianna that I can, and I try to pray often the prayers she wrote down and left us, like this one: *Jesus, I promise You to submit myself to all that You permit to befall me, make me only know Your will.*

Short but sweet, Saint Gianna's prayer reminds us of just what it is we're all really called to do. The trick is that she does so in a way that we're not very accustomed to—not as a medieval monk or priestly ascetic, but rather as a wife, doctor, and mom.

A BLAST FROM THE PAST

Surprisingly enough, this devotion to modern saints has actually made saints from an earlier time much more attractive. One who has become really important for me is Saint Rita of Cascia. She, along with Saint Jude the Apostle, is known as a patron of impossible causes, and as my wife could well tell you, I'm about as impossible as they come. More than that, though, Rita was known, even during her lifetime, as a great worker of wonders. And who doesn't need a wonder worked in their life? I invite you to read her life as well as those of the many other saints of old, and see just how their example and witness to Jesus Christ can change your and your family's lives.

LIKE A FAMILY REUNION

Getting to know our older and newer brothers and sisters in the communion of saints and picking out our own personal heroes and intercessors from among them can be a bit like getting to know our families. Remember as a kid first learning what cousins were, but then trying to match the cousins with the aunts and uncles? And then later trying to figure out which aunt or uncle belonged to Mom or Dad? And what about all those people who weren't actually related or were very distantly related but whom we called "Grandma" or "Uncle"? Well, getting to know the saints is a lot like that. These people are already related to us in the faith, but we have to figure out how and why, and what importance they're going to have in the rest of our lives.

Though the three saints whom I mentioned are all Italian, that doesn't mean that I'm only drawn to saints from the same place as my ancestors. We can all find different ways of relating to saints, just as we relate to people in our families for different reasons. For most of us, there's a special closeness between siblings that usually doesn't happen between, say, first cousins. If you were named after a saint they should hold a kind of necessary place for you in your daily prayer, afterall you are named *after* them. .

Getting to know the stories of their lives, or at least the stories of why your parents chose your name for you, can awaken us to the special virtues of these great saints, as we, hopefully, follow suit. Confirmation saints are also people that we should hold a special affection for as they were chosen (most likely by us) as people that we admired. If you simply chose one for no other reason than you liked his or her name, then read about them now. It's never too late to make new friends!

Then there are those cousins, aunts, or uncles to whom we're not especially closely related, but with whom we share a special interest. This is where patron saints can really come in handy. Saint Sebastian, for instance, is the patron saint of athletes, so if you're an athlete he might be someone to relate to. Saint Dominic is the patron of astronomers, Saint Albert the sciences in general, Saint Paul of writers, Saint Vitus of dancers, and so on. Other patronages work because of particular situations. Saint Lucy, for example, is invoked when people have eye trouble, Saint Apollonia for teeth problems, and Saint Gerard and Saint Gianna for pregnant mothers. The good news is that you can't ever have too many patron saints, and they never get jealous of each other. Maybe you're a dancer but you also have trouble with your teeth; praying each day to Saint Vitus and Saint Apollonia is probably a very good idea. Likewise, if you're a writer who has trouble with your eyes, Saint Paul and Saint Lucy will make a dynamic duo.

I often find that lesser-known saints are the most compelling in my own life. For example, I was trying to help a friend dealing with some serious depression and family issues to find a saint to bring all of that to. Then I just happened to visit the Shrine of Our Lady of the Snows in Bellville, IL. The shrine is run by the Oblates of Mary Immaculate, a religious order founded by Saint Eugene de Mazenod. There were profound issues in Saint

Eugene's family life, including mental and emotional illness, instability, infidelity, and possibly even domestic abuse. And yet despite his supremely dysfunctional family Eugene went on to become a terrifically successful religious founder and bishop. He was a natural choice as a patron saint for my friend.

The point is that the whole raft of aunts, uncles, cousins, and the like that God has given us in the Church can lead to a host of relationships that would otherwise be impossible. This is important because it goes right to the heart of why we believe in the communion of saints at all, and what it ultimately means for all of us. Holiness really is possible for us all, but my holiness won't look like Padre Pio's, or Saint Rita's, or even Bl. Gianna's. My holiness will be my own, born of my relationship with God, nurtured by the sacraments, and expressed as that of a husband and father in the twenty-first century. What will yours be?

A GREAT CLOUD OF WITNESSES

If a contemporary Catholic critique of devotion to the saints is "Well, what do they have to do with me?" then a classic Protestant objection is "Well, what do they have to do with Jesus?" No small amount of ink and sometimes even blood has been spilled on the topic. One of the problems seems to be that devotion to the saints, and to Mary in particular, is so basic a response on the part of Catholics and Orthodox Christians that nobody before the Reformation seemed to even think to object to the practice. But in the responses that we can offer to our Protestant friends in trying to explain our practice of venerating the saints, I think we can see something of why doing so is so vital and important to our spiritual life.

So, your Protestant friend says to you over coffee one evening, or maybe after a wake where a rosary was said, "Why do you guys worship Mary and the saints?" Sighing, you calmly explain that we don't "worship" anybody but God, but that we "venerate" Mary and all the saints as friends of God and therefore those closest to him in heaven. You may even be quick enough to point out that in a prayer like the Hail Mary, the only thing we ask Mary to do is "pray for us sinners now, and at the hour of death." Requests for prayers from living people are obviously all right, so why not from those dead people whom we know to be in a much better position to make those prayers anyhow?

But your friend points out that necromancy was forbidden in the Old Testament. You don't even know what necromancy is, so he explains that it is the practice of consorting with the dead, like what the Witch of Endor did with the ghost of Samuel in 1 Samuel 28. Soothsaying and divination and the like are certainly forbidden, but you point out that communicating with the dead can't be ruled out absolutely since God has at times permitted it, like when he allowed Moses and Elijah to speak with Jesus on the mountain before Peter, James, and John. The point is that using occult practices to conjure up spirits is a problem, but obviously a widowed husband looking at his wife's picture and asking her to pray to God for him in his pain is a very different thing than going to a medium to try and communicate with her spirit.

What's more, the Scriptures explicitly point to the prayers of the saints, especially in the book of Revelation. Here the prayers of the saints are identified with bowls of incense that burn night and day before God. Little kids often ask (and grown-ups too, but more quietly), "What do we do in heaven all the time?" The answer is there in Revelation: We pray. And who among us, once we get to heaven, wouldn't have loads of people to remember back here on earth? In fact, it is precisely their physical proximity to God (which the image from Revelation is trying to show) that allows them both to hear our prayers and to offer prayers on our behalf.

But the more fundamental objection, "What do they have to do with Jesus?" is actually very important. We can think of the saints in a whole variety of ways—as holy people, as the deceased gone before us in faith, as examples of the spiritual life and all the rest—but most fundamentally, they are friends of God in Christ. They are the friends of Jesus who, as they depart this life, are brought into even closer communion with him. This is what makes venerating the saints, getting to know them, learning from their lives and witness, and relying heavily on their prayer so natural to the Christian people. We draw near the saints because they are the friends of Christ, and just as the friends of our friends become our friends in turn, the friends of Jesus, from whatever time and place and background, are to be our friends too.

NOBODY GETS THERE ALONE

The phrase might seem cheesy, but I've never forgotten it. The priest at my college learned it from one of the sisters who taught him in grade school, who'd have them all sit in a circle and would say, "See, kids, this is what heaven is like." Confused, the children would look from one to another. "Nobody gets there alone," she'd continue. "But they're holding hands with the person next to them the whole way along." This is a thoroughly Catholic sentiment: My relationship with Jesus needs to be personal, but it can never be truly private. The personal relationship is one of intimacy and encounter with the living God from our hearts. And with that intimacy comes a desire for us to share whom it is we love with others, thus never making our faith private. We live in relation to others, both here on earth and in heaven. And the people we share this life with matter, so we have an obligation to get to know them, to tend to them as best we're able, and to rely on them as much as we can.

So what should devotion to the saints look like in your family and in your life? Well, it's hard to say. Each of us has our own needs and backgrounds and practices, but the following are some fairly standard ways that a lot of people draw life and love from their participation in the communion of saints.

First of all, start reading saints' lives. I know it sounds hokey, and that you might even be embarrassed to run to your local Catholic bookstore and buy one, but they really make a difference. In fact, historically, hagiography (saint biographies) has been the most consistently popular genre of biographies, not just among Christians, but among all people. At times reading or learning about saints' lives has actually been more popular than reading the Scriptures. While most of the saints themselves would be uncomfortable with having their lives take precedence over that of our Lord's, the deeper intuition here is that the saints, by their very lives, show us what it means to be a Christian and so how to live with Jesus each day. In that way, saints' lives are really just the ongoing story of Jesus's life and how it lives in and among his people. Seriously, start reading them. Maybe start with some more contemporary holy people like Bl. Pope John Paul II or Bl. Mother Teresa of Calcutta. Or maybe you could start by reading the Acts of the Apostles to get a sense of some of those early saints in the Church. Whatever you choose, there are loads of resources available through your parish, your public library, and the Internet. There are dozens of e-books available for little to no cost. A good place to start is Alban Butler's *Lives of the Saints,* which has been for a long time a much read text.

One good way to get into saints' lives is to read them to your kids. It's never too early to start talking to your children about the saints, and there are literally hundreds of good books designed specifically for little ones about the saints and their lives with God. Telling your children about their patron saints or how you picked their names is also really important. This is why the ancient custom of giving Christian children explicitly Christian names is so vital. It gives them both constant intercessors and role models to emulate. Even if, for some reason, you feel compelled to give your children names not explicitly associated with any saint, pick special patrons for them from the beginning. At their baptisms entrust them to those saints' care and watchful protection, and tell them the stories of their heavenly intercessors as they grow.

Think about telling the stories of the lives of the saints in the same way you would tell your kids the stories of the lives of their grandparents and extended family. Just as you might say, "Well now, this is how your grandma got here from . . ." so also you might say, "Well you know, this is how the faith got brought to Ireland . . ." These stories form us and give us a sense of identity and purpose. Your children will only benefit, and you will too, from having to study the stories well enough to tell them.

Finally, always be on the lookout for saints in your own life and the life of the Church around you. As I wrote earlier, in my own home state of Iowa there is a great move to get the first priest assigned to the state, Fr. Samuel Mazzuchelli, O.P., canonized. Most places may not have someone with an official cause in the Church, but they often do have a much revered pastor long dead, or a pious old lady known for the effectiveness of her prayers alive in the hearts of the people. And as you remember the dead of your own families, don't neglect to ask their prayers for you. If

Grandma and Grandpa are in heaven, then they're a lot closer to the Lord than you are right now, so use them as best you can, and teach your kids to do the same.

THAT'S WHAT IT'S ALL ABOUT

The saints are our intercessors, family, and friends, and they are also the signs of what we are to become if we remain faithful. It's important to give our kids and grandkids good role models and to teach them to rely upon their intercession. It's also important to remind them of their ultimate goal, and our ultimate goal: to become a saint. This, in the end, will help make everything else make sense. It will also allow us, in what we say and, more fundamentally, in what we do, to spread this good news of Jesus Christ, not only in our families and in our parishes, but in our neighborhoods, towns, and indeed the whole world.

MOTHER KNOWS BEST

No book on Catholic family life would be complete without something dedicated in a very special way to the Blessed Mother. Of course, this whole book has been dedicated to her in one way or another, but she is such a central part of the devotional and spiritual life of every Catholic family and parish, and every Christian in general, whether they realize it or not, that I simply couldn't call the book "done" without saying something more directly about her role in our lives and the model she unceasingly provides.

"But wait a sec, Jon," you might be saying. "I'm a good Catholic and don't have a very strong devotion to Mary. And the rosary and stuff like that is all optional, right?" Well, kind of. We're certainly not obliged to any particular devotion by the Church's law in the way that we are to attend Mass on Sundays and holy days, for example, but it's hard to imagine a Catholic able to live a real and vital spiritual life without some kind of devotional component. It would be a bit like a person trying to lose weight who dieted a lot but never exercised. The diet helps you not accumulate more, but the exercise helps you lose what fat you already have.

And the intercession of the saints isn't optional. Sometimes when we're answering Protestant objections to the veneration of the saints we'll say things like "Statues and icons help us to pray," and "Praying to Mary isn't required in the way that praying to Jesus is," and those things are both true—again, kind of. But whenever the Church gathers to celebrate Mass it invokes the Blessed Virgin by name and relies on her intercession, in the most sacred prayer of all—that which consecrates the Eucharist. Listen for it next time at Mass. All of the other saints are optional, but she's not. And at the most critical sacramental moments of a Christian's life—baptism, confirmation, marriage, ordination, anointing—a litany invoking particular saints is usually said. And you know who's always first? You got it—Our Lady. So devotion to the saints isn't really an option, at least in the sense that one can easily opt out of it, and a special love for Mary is absolutely essential.

The worry is, of course, that devotion to the saints can lead to somehow slighting God. But this is kind of like worrying that love for you is going to prevent other people from loving your mother. In our experience just the opposite is the case. The more people grow to love you, the more they appreciate, revere, and love your parents. That's the ancient Christian intuition behind devotion to Mary: Love of the mother leads to even greater love of her son.

Saint Louis de Montfort, one of the greatest preachers ever on Our Lady, used to say, "The mother always points to the son." This insight comes directly from the Scriptures. At the wedding at Cana, in Galilee, Mary asks Jesus for a favor. He gives her a somewhat strange response: *"Woman, how does your concern affect me?"* But she is not put off; she goes to the servants and says, *"Do whatever He tells you."* (John 2:22) Now, I don't know about you, but that is not how my mother would respond if I said to her, "Woman!" Of course, Mary understands, or at least trusts, that because of who Jesus is he will come through for her. The reason he calls her "woman" is not because he is in any way disrespecting her—in fact it is the exact opposite. It is because he is referring to her as the new Eve. Her yes to the angel Gabriel to bear the Son of God to the world undoes the great no of the first woman, Eve, in the garden. Mary's obedience and her instruction to obey is the response that the first man and the first woman failed to give in their disobedience. Jesus's use of *woman* in reference to his own mother is the greatest title of respect and devotion he could offer her, because she truly is the new model of womanhood and humanity that will finally help to resolve our relationship with God. This is what she does for us, and it is why, in her words, deeds, and prayers, the Blessed Mother really does know best.

ISN'T JESUS ENOUGH?

Sometimes you'll hear Evangelicals say things like, "Well, isn't Jesus enough?" The answer is, of course, "Yes, but that's not the point." It's because Jesus is enough for all of our desires, enough to satisfy all of our longings, enough to save us, enough to redeem us, and enough to transform us into more than we could have ever imagined on our own that Mary matters at all. Mary exists for us only in relation to her son, which should tell us something important about how we are to relate not only to Mary, but to Jesus as well.

Jesus is enough because of the Incarnation. He is the "Man from Heaven," the God-Man sent to earth to save us. The loud cry of the early Church is echoed in Thomas the Apostle's recognition of the risen Jesus: *"My Lord and my God!"* (John 20:28) Jesus is enough because he is both true God and true man. The unity of Jesus's person is what accomplishes our salvation and sanctifies human nature. Before Jesus we were all sons and daughters of God, but only as a kind of metaphor because God had created us.

In Jesus we are all sons and daughters of God really, actually, and truly, but by adoption. Jesus shares this relationship with God through the Incarnation and redemption with us so that we can become like him and relate to God even as he does.

But awe at the person of Jesus can have the effect of making him less accessible. Though the Incarnation was meant to make God more accessible to us, and in fact did so in more ways than we can possibly understand, most of us at some point think of Jesus in the midst of some kind of moral problem and say, "Yeah, but he was God, so of course he could get it right." Mary, of course, was not God. There is nothing divine about Mary except her son, and she did not give him his divinity. Rather, the Divine One from all eternity chose her from among all women to be his mother. That, if nothing else, should tell us something important about why we should love Mary.

THE WORLD'S FIRST LOVE

Archbishop Fulton J. Sheen, the famous television preacher of the middle twentieth century, used to call the Blessed Virgin "the world's first love." What he meant by this was that Mary, as the most perfect woman who had ever lived, was really the archetype or original plan of every love that we've ever had. She is the whole world's love, because she is God's first love, the creature he loves best of all, and the one he chose for all eternity to be the mother of God the Son.

She is the world's first love because despite having been born in time herself, everything that she is, was born to be, and became was what the world had always longed for. The angel calls her "full of grace," and we echo his greeting every time we say the Hail Mary (Luke 1:28). The Greek word used here in the New Testament is *kecharitomene*, which means something like "so full of grace that there's not room for anything else." Mary was so caught up in relationship with God that there simply wasn't room for anything else. She is the world's first love because she is God's first love, and she is God's first love because she so loves God.

Mary is also the world's best love, because she loves the world best. Mary's love for God was perfect, because she loved God not only as the father and protector of Israel, but also as her son and her spouse. She knew God as intimately as any creature ever has: She bore him in her womb, nursed him at her breast, changed his diapers and soothed his rash. She kissed his skinned knees and made him his favorite treats, consoled him when life was hard and laughed with him when life was best. She stood with him, even when she did not understand him, and walked with him all the way to the cross—and beyond. Even those special graces that we talk about as hers alone, the Immaculate Conception and the Assumption, are only because of her relationship to him. Her conception was immaculate—that is, from the moment that she came into existence in her mother's womb, she was completely without original sin, because from the first moment of her existence God wanted to keep her pure, holy, and his. Her Assumption is a share in her son's Resurrection, and a sign to us of what awaits each of us at the end of time. Her relationship, her love of God in her son, was real, palpable, even fleshly, and so it was best. Our own love should also be born of blood, sweat, and tears, and that will make us best and most like her. And through her, we will be better able imitate him.

A HOLY FAMILY

Despite all of the accolades given her by Christians throughout history, in her own lifetime Mary was probably one of the most maligned women in history. She was an unwed teenage mother, taken in by a poor laborer. She was a refugee before her child was even born, and an immigrant while her son was still in infancy. Even Saint Joseph believed that she'd cheated on him at first, which is probably an important lesson for us about judgment and the truthfulness of a lot of our conclusions. By all accounts the family continued to live in poverty, and even when they returned to Nazareth years later, the shadow of that early scandal must have followed her wherever she went.

Mary is a sign for us of the kind of holiness of which we are all capable, even (and maybe especially) in the midst of difficult situations. Think about the pregnant teenager you see in the back pew at Mass, or the man at work whose wife seems a little crazy. Consider the immigrant who accidentally backs into your car and doesn't have insurance, or the beggars who sit outside your favorite store. These are not simply people to be pitied or prayed for, with no real hope for their futures. They are potentially saints, even great saints, and we should treat them as such.

Of course, it was not simply the poverty or the difficulties experienced by the Holy Family that made them holy. It was their love of God that bound them all together. Saint Joseph too, living with Mary and the Christ child, grew in his love both of her and of Jesus, as well as of his other children, relatives, friends, and customers. This Christian charity thing begins at home but winds up being pretty all-encompassing. Your love for your spouse and your kids should make you love your customers more or your boss better. It should result, at the very least, in your being kind to the janitor and courteous to the cleaning lady. But in the end, it should ultimately make the both of you better—more holy.

LADY OF SORROW, LADY OF JOY

Our Lady's life was a hard one, to be sure, harder than most of us ever have it—but it was also better. Putting God into the human equation ups the ante higher than we can imagine on our own. Our sorrows become even more tragic, and our joys become even more ecstatic. Mary knew deeply, intimately, as close to perfectly as humans are able, all the best and worst bits of humanity.

The Church traditionally names "Seven Joys" and "Seven Sorrows" of Our Lady. These are really just ways of organizing the major events in Mary's life, but they are good material for our meditation because in their own way, they come to impact and parallel each of our lives as well.

The Seven Sorrows of the Blessed Virgin are: the Prophecy of Simeon, the Flight into Egypt, the Loss of the Child Jesus in the Temple, Mary Meeting Jesus on the Way to Calvary, The Death of Jesus, Mary Receiving the Body of Jesus into Her Arms, and the Burial of Jesus. Think about these for a second. What parent wants to be told something horrible about their child on the day of his baptism? But this is essentially what happened in the Temple with Simeon the Prophet. Or imagine the fear of Mary as the family was forced to flee into Egypt, and imagine the countless refugee mothers with their infant children in camps throughout the world, or the immigrant women in our own country terrified in homeless shelters and migrant settlements. And what parent having lost their child at the store or the mall doesn't identify with Mary and Joseph when the child goes missing at the temple? Who among us hasn't heard a parent who has lost a child say that it truly is the worst thing on earth? Why do you think the *Pietà* is the most visited statue in the world? The Blessed Mother cradles her dead son in her arms, even as she once cradled the cooing infant. Who among us can stop from weeping at the Mother of the Universe weeping at the death of her son and Lord?

But the life of Mary was not only sorrow. Therefore the joys are worth praying over too, lest we begin to see our own lives only in terms of sadness. The Seven Joys of Mary are: the Annunciation, the Nativity of Jesus, the Adoration of the Magi, the Resurrection of Christ, the Ascension of Christ to Heaven, the Pentecost or Decent of the Holy Spirit upon the Apostles and Mary, and the Coronation of the Virgin in Heaven. Now, some of these are perhaps less obviously relatable than those in the first list, which may be the reason we tend to talk about them less, but the point is clearly the same. The sorrows of Mary were eclipsed only by her own joys, and her joys were perfected in that great and final mystery that we call her coronation; for she is queen of heaven and of earth.

POEMS, PRAYERS, AND PROMISES

The rosary is far and away the most common devotion, not only to Mary, but in the whole Church. If you have a rosary take it out now. Look at it carefully. Maybe it's delicate and pretty, much like Our Lady, to whom it is dedicated. Maybe it's rough-looking and tough. She was too, in her own way. One of my favorite paintings is called The Assumption. It's really just a picture of Saint John looking up into the sky, but we can see Mary's foot at the top of the painting. The foot is old and gnarled, not the way we usually think of her, but if she'd lived that long and had that hard a life, her feet would probably look like your grandmother's—not obviously pretty, but in a much deeper way one of the most beautiful things on earth. Maybe this is why the Prophet said, *"How beautiful are the feet of those who on the mountain bring good news."* (Isaiah 52:7)

We tend to think of the rosary as an old person's prayer, a pious addiction for worrisome people. I think, though, that part of the appeal of the rosary is its universality. Sure, pious old ladies thumb their beads before Mass every morning, but soldiers will pocket stones in their trousers or finger ridges on their rings while in the trenches. The Dominicans added the rosary to their habit, wearing it on their belts, precisely because it was to take the place of their swords. The rosary can be a tough prayer, and if the lives of the saints are to be believed, it is one of the most potent weapons against the wickedness of Satan.

A great story is told about Hilaire Belloc, an English Catholic who served in Parliament in the early twentieth century. There was a lot of debate during his campaign about his Catholicism. Once during a campaign speech someone started to heckle him over his faith and he pulled out a rosary and said something like, "Sir, so far as possible I hear Mass each day and I go to my knees and tell these beads each night. If that offends you, then I pray God may spare me the indignity of representing you in Parliament." The rosary can be a manly prayer just as surely as it can be a feminine one, which is one of the most important reasons to pray it with your family.

It happened to me once that a friend who is not Catholic got on me for praying my rosary. He cited Jesus's famous admonition concerning the Gentiles, who "suppose that they will be heard for their many words," (Matt. 6:7) while explaining to me just how boring it must be to say the same thing over and over again. While we were speaking, his child came up and hugged him, saying, "Daddy, I love you!" And so I asked him, "How many times a day does she say that?" He smiled and said, "Dozens." I then said, "Well doesn't that get old, hearing her recite the same thing over and over and over again? Perhaps even boring you?" He of course said no. So I went on, "Well, that's what the rosary is like. Each bead we're just saying again and again and again, to Mary and to Jesus and to all the saints, but mostly to God himself, 'I love you! I love you! I love you!'"

Praying the rosary with your family is like teaching your kids to say, "I love you." It's true, they won't always like it. Sometimes they'll get bored. Sometimes they won't mean it. But mostly, and over time, they will. It's the same as teaching kids to say please and thank you. It will stick, and they'll learn to mean it. And "I love you" means much, much more than please and thank you.

The rosary is a string of poems, prayers, and promises, a chain of hope and a kind of umbilical cord to heaven. We turn to Mary so that we can turn better to the Son, and in the very turning we are ourselves changed. We have a serious obligation to teach our kids many things, and of course to take them to Mass, but teaching your kids the rosary, making sure they keep one in their pocket, and praying it together as a family if not every day, at least sometimes or even just a decade here or there, will make all the difference in the world.

Because its origins lie in the back-and-forth singing of the Psalms in church, one of the best ways to pray the rosary is together. If you haven't prayed the rosary together as a family, I wouldn't necessarily recommend sitting your six-year-old down and trying to blitz the whole thing just after dinner. But a decade or two before bed each night can be a good way to start. And the rosary as a family prayer shouldn't be confined just to your own family. Your parish family should gather to say the rosary too, and this will help accustom your kids to it. Nose around at your local church and see if they have a rosary before or after one of the Masses. If not, why not start one? Obviously talk to the pastor first, but so long as you are sincere and not too pushy he should be more than happy to accommodate you. Don't be intimidated—there are a host of resources available to help people pray over and meditate upon the mysteries. There are some programs even designed specifically for kids. And talk to other families and friends. Maybe staying after church ten minutes will give the people downstairs just enough time to prep the coffee and doughnuts so they don't have to leave Mass early! However you work it out, pray the rosary; pray it alone, pray it together, pray it often, and pray it well.

MOTHERHOOD AND APPLE PIE

We associate motherhood with comfort and goodness and sweet things. But mothers are also tough and strong and very, very brave. Our Blessed Mother is probably the best model of this, and like our own mothers at their best, she makes us better too. She is always there as an advocate, a coach, a sounding board, and a soft place to land. Take advantage of what she has to offer, and teach your kids to as well. Whether you recognize it or not, she's already one of the most important members of your family, and your kids should know so too.

Cultivate a true devotion to Mary in your homes. Place her image around the house. Say the rosary together as a family, at least sometimes. Teach your kids to pray for her intercession before tests and ball games and plays and concerts. Refer to her example of purity and holiness and goodwill. Make sure the kids know that she's sweet and kind and good, but also strong and brave and very, very holy. Make this combination a kind of model for them to follow. Let them know that she is the first and best disciple and so our best model to follow Jesus. But also make sure they know that she is the Mother of the Church, our advocate, protector, and guide. Keep a rosary in your pocket or under your pillow. Thumb your beads when you don't know what else to do, just as your kids sometimes crawl up into your lap and tell you they love you, just because that's what they were made to do. It's what you were made to do too.

STAR OF THE NEW EVANGELIZATION

It was Blessed Pope John Paul II who first called for a new evangelization. He compared the work of today's Christians to those who first had to bring the Faith to a foreign land. So many of the people with whom we live and work, even members of our own extended families, simply know little to nothing of the faith. It's like reinventing the wheel. And so our work is long. And hard. And difficult. And it can be tempting at times to give up.

But Mary, like a good mother, reminds us not to. She is our mother, holding us tight, kissing our boo-boos, and setting us right. She is a consoling presence in all of our lives and a mothering influence during our most difficult trials. She prays for us and takes care of us and makes sure that, in the end, we take care of one another.

But she is only our mother because she is first his mother. As the mother of Jesus, who is God, Mary is the only person who is present at all times in the history of salvation: before Christ, during his life and ministry, and in the life of the Church. Her maternal presence and care precede all evangelization, first because it is she who brings him who is announced into the world, but even more because it is her great love for those who do not yet know of her son that wins for them the great gift of the gospel's proclamation. When a new religious order is founded, there is usually some sort of a story about Mary having prayed to her son for some very specific cause, and the answer to the prayer is the new religious community.

Mary has a host of titles, but the most important for us today is Star of the New Evangelization. In the ancient Church she was called the Morning Star because she preceded the dawn, who is Christ. In the new evangelization she is the star on the horizon that gives us, her children, direction and hope. She is the sign to us that we will be successful in our efforts. She is the comfort that assures us in our doubts. She is the model that we both imitate and hold out to others. And she is the great and constant intercessor with her son. You are reading this book today because of her prayers for you, and insofar as you are able to bring your family to deeper faith, it will be because of her prayers. In the end, it will be Our Lady who brings us, and all those whom our lives touch, to her son. And it will be with her that we will celebrate, all of us together, in the presence of the living God.

So turn to her in your own missionary efforts as a family. Ask her to help you see how you can be better wives, better husbands, better parents, better children, better teachers, and better witnesses to the world. Let Mary be the lodestar, the sign in the star by which you and your family set your course. Let her be your family's example, always pointing you toward the way of humility and the desires of her son. Let her be your family's intercessor, praying always for you and for the success of your mission, together, but most important as a member of the Catholic Church. And always and everywhere seek her intercession. Some of the most effective preachers I know always pray a rosary before they begin. Calling upon Mary in the midst of those situations that are most difficult to be witnesses to, and with those people who try us most, is our best and only chance of bringing about the conversion we desire so much, and that we so desperately need.

Conclusion

We started this all with a question: What is your family for? I hope that by now you have something of an answer, or at least something closer to an answer than you might have had before. We know the challenges that lie before us, the difficulties that society presents to us, and the doubts and fears that plague all of us. But hopefully after prayerfully considering what's in this book you've been able to see a way forward. Hopefully you understand better now why your family is so important, why you and your spouse and your kids are absolutely invaluable to the life of the Church and the future of humanity, and most important, why you are the best agents of change the Church has at her disposal.

There's not much new in this book. It's all stuff that you could find without too much effort thumbing through the Scriptures and the *Catechism*. There's theory and practice, helpful hints and inspiring anecdotes, stories that teach and examples that show us how to be better Christians. But hopefully there's something more as well. Hopefully in reading this book you have at least been able to taste something of the faith that burns deep inside me, of the hope that I hold out for your family and for mine, and of the great love that I bear not only toward our Church and her traditions, but toward the world in such desperate need of us now as never before.

You are part of a family, a family that extends beyond your immediate relations. Your primary responsibilities are and must remain your spouse, your kids, and those closest to you. But in your care for them, in the way that you continue to grow together in holiness, you must never forget that you are part of a greater family. Your local parish is a sign of it, but even it is only a part of a much greater whole. You are members of a body, a body of believers united in faith, hope, and charity under the sign of the cross and in the name of the Lord Jesus. This community is bound by blood, but not yours or mine; rather, the precious blood of Christ. This blood has won for us not only a ransom from sin and death, but a new lease on life. We are free now like never before. And in our freedom we must love as none has ever loved.

So take whatever wisdom you can from these pages. Understand your faith better and be inspired to go and learn even more. Read the Scriptures and study the *Catechism* and other Church documents. Pray more and receive the sacraments with greater devotion and faith. Increase your devotion to Mary and the saints and get to know even better your local parish and diocese. Introduce your children to as much as you can. Play games with them. Pray with them. Teach them how to pray, and how to love, and how to forgive. Remind them of their great dignity as Christian men and women. Show them what powerful agents of change they can be in the Church and in the world.

And as you move forward, don't neglect where you've come from. Remember your parents and siblings and relatives and friends who may have wound up in a very different place, who may be far removed from the life of the Church. Don't forget them. Share your faith—not just the content, but the experience. Tell the story of how the Lord has changed your life and your family's life, and help people see how God can do the same for them.

And most of all, dear readers, have great confidence. There is no program here, no workbook to complete, no class to sign up for. This is just what living life as a faithful Catholic means. Remember me, and all those who journey with you in faith, who work alongside you with great hope, and who long to see the fruits of our labor—a world filled with the great love of Christ for his Church, the Church that has given us all new birth by water and the Spirit, and the Church in which we still proclaim the good news that Christ has come to save us all.

Your mission, should you choose to accept it, is to be a missionary. Just as in olden times, Jesus today sends his friends out two by two, sharing his love with all we meet. He's sending you with your spouse and your kids, with your parents and siblings, your neighbors and friends and fellow parishoners. He's sending you out with and to all people of goodwill to proclaim the good news that has changed your life and that can change their lives as well: Jesus Christ is Lord! He wants you to be a part of it. He wants your mission to be his own. He wants you to help him in the greatest of adventures, the hard work of saving the world.

About the Author

For the past five years Jon Leonetti has dedicated his life to engaging Catholics in all walks of life. Providing keynote presentations and parish missions internationally, Jon is a recognized leader in the Church today, helping others to cultivate intimacy with Jesus Christ through prayer, Sacraments, family life, Mary and the saints.

Jon and his wife Teresa reside in Des Moines, Iowa with their son Joseph. Jon is currently pursuing a masters degree in moral theology from Holy Apostles College and Seminary.

To schedule Jon to come speak at your parish, or event, email: Jon.Leonetti@gmail.com or go online: www.JDLeonetti.com

THE DYNAMIC CATHOLIC
CONFIRMATION EXPERIENCE

"I am convinced this is the best invitation to young Catholics to accept and live their faith that I have encountered."

— CARDINAL DONALD WUERL, Archbishop of Washington

REQUEST YOUR FREE* PROGRAM PACK
at DynamicCatholic.com/Confirmation

*The complimentary program pack includes:
the complete DVD series containing 72 short films,
the student workbook, and the leader guide.*

*Just pay shipping.

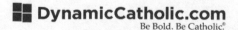

DynamicCatholic.com
Be Bold. Be Catholic.®

NOTES

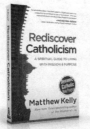

NOTES

NOTES

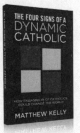

NOTES

THE
DYNAMIC CATHOLIC
INSTITUTE

[MISSION]

To re-energize the Catholic Church
in America by developing world-class
resources that inspire people to
rediscover the genius of Catholicism.

[VISION]

To be the innovative leader in the
New Evangelization helping Catholics
and their parishes become
the-best-version-of-themselves.

DynamicCatholic.com
Be Bold. Be Catholic.®

The Dynamic Catholic Institute
5081 Olympic Blvd
Erlanger, KY 41018
Phone: 859-980-7900
info@DynamicCatholic.com